TRACING YOUR PRE-VICTORIAN ANCESTORS

A Guide to Research Methods for Family Historians

John Wintrip

Pen & Sword

First published in Great Britain in 2017
PEN & SWORD FAMILY HISTORY
an imprint of
Pen & Sword Books Ltd
47 Church Street,
Barnsley
South Yorkshire,
S70 2AS

ISBN 978 1 47388 065 8

A CIP catalogue record for this book is
available from the British Library.

Typeset in Palatino and Optima by CHIC GRAPHICS

Printed and bound in England by
CPI Group (UK), Croydon, CR0 4YY

Pen & Sword Books Ltd incorporates the imprints of Pen & Sword
Archaeology, Atlas, Aviation, Battleground, Discovery, Family History,
History, Maritime, Military, Naval, Politics, Railways, Select, Social History,
Transport, True Crime, Claymore Press, Frontline Books, Leo Cooper,
Praetorian Press, Remember When, Seaforth Publishing and Wharncliffe.

For a complete list of Pen & Sword titles please contact
PEN & SWORD BOOKS LTD
47 Church Street, Barnsley, South Yorkshire, S70 2AS, England
E-mail: enquiries@pen-and-sword.co.uk
Website: www.pen-and-sword.co.uk

CONTENTS

ACKNOWLEDGEMENTS

I would like to express my thanks to my wife Jessica for her support while I was writing this book, all my clients for providing me with the opportunity to research their ancestors, and the staff of the large number of archives throughout the country where I have carried out both personal and professional research over many years. I would also like to register my gratitude to Karina Williamson, Malcolm McEachran and Susan Moore for reading through drafts of the text and making valuable suggestions.

ABBREVIATIONS

The following abbreviations have been used throughout this book:

GRO   General Register Office
LDS   Church of Jesus Christ of Latter-day Saints
                (Mormons)
SoG   Society of Genealogists
TNA   The National Archives

INTRODUCTION

Civil registration was introduced in England and Wales on 1 July 1837. Queen Victoria had ascended the throne only a few days earlier on 20 June, so the period before civil registration can very conveniently be referred to as the pre-Victorian period. I have written this book to offer guidance to family historians tracing their English ancestors in the pre-Victorian period, when research becomes more challenging than after 1837 because church registers recorded less genealogical information than civil registration records and information on exact birthplace from census records is only available for those people who were still alive and living in Great Britain in 1851. The focus of this book is genealogical research in England, where most of my personal and professional research has been carried out, but the same principles are also applicable to Wales, as the systems of record-keeping in the two countries were virtually identical.

Although this is a book for family historians, it is concerned with genealogy in the traditional sense of establishing relationships between generations, as it is essential to ensure that the correct individual or family has been identified before undertaking any wider investigation of family history. In any case the distinction between genealogy and family history in the pre-Victorian period becomes increasingly blurred as a result of the more limited range of sources available.

Genealogical research involves seeking previously unknown information about specific people, usually concerning the identity of their spouse or parents, and research on each ancestral line proceeds backwards in time in a sequence of logical steps. Some steps may be relatively straightforward, whereas others are difficult or impossible, and the term *brick wall* is often used to describe the latter category. A brick wall will eventually be encountered for each ancestral line, but some apparent brick walls are temporary obstacles that can be overcome through knowledge of relevant sources and the use of appropriate search tools and research techniques, as well as incorporating external background knowledge to interpret the information in those records that have been found and to identify further sources.

The classic work on genealogical research in England published during the twentieth century, still sometimes found on library shelves, was *Genealogical Research in England and Wales*, by Gardner and Smith, published in Salt Lake City in three volumes between 1956 and 1964. These volumes were written primarily to assist members of the LDS to research their English and Welsh ancestry at a time when genealogy still had a rather elitist image on this side of the Atlantic, where it was widely perceived as an esoteric and scholarly pursuit for the leisured classes rather than a leisure pursuit for the masses. Genealogy in the traditional sense of constructing pedigrees was only beginning to be transformed into family history as we now understand it, most parish registers were still held in churches, computers with far less processing power than smartphones filled whole rooms, and local family history societies were yet to be established. Nonetheless, the third volume in this set of books (Gardner and Smith, 1964) includes chapters on research procedures that are still relevant today.

Many books on genealogy have been published since the 1960s, but almost all have focused on sources. While still an amateur researcher I noticed that despite the plethora of books describing the sources in which I could potentially find information about my ancestors, very little information was included on how to do research, although Rogers (2008), first published in 1983, adopts a problem-solving approach, and many case studies illustrating sound genealogical research methods can be found scattered in books and magazine articles. I gradually came to the conclusion that this dearth of guidance was partly because genealogical research is far too complex to be reduced to a set of simple instructions, and partly because only a relatively small number of people, mainly professional genealogists with many years' experience of carrying out research for clients with ancestors from a wide range of backgrounds, are likely to have the breadth of experience necessary to write books specifically on this topic.

The first book on genealogical research methods to be published for almost half a century appeared in 2012, written by professional genealogist Helen Osborn (Osborn, 2012). *Genealogy: Essential Research Methods* provides an excellent introduction, but I felt that a book for more advanced researchers focusing specifically on the period before civil registration was also needed. Not being aware of anyone else planning to write such a book I began contemplating doing so myself. Although I had not previously written any books for publication, during my earlier career as a librarian in universities I had written many explanatory guides for library users. While recognizing the impossibility of reducing genealogical research to a set of simple instructions, I thought it might still be possible to produce a useful book summarizing the most important principles and highlighting common errors. I began to make notes on topics I thought should be included, based on insights from my personal and professional research, taking into account the kind of background information I have included in reports for clients, questions clients have asked and unsound assumptions they have made, as well as errors I made myself as a novice researcher. My ideas for the contents of a book developed over several years, and when I approached Pen & Sword with my proposal they were keen for me to proceed.

Solving genealogical problems before 1837 often requires using resources available online in combination with original sources and search tools located in specific archives and libraries. I have encountered researchers who have spent many hours searching for information in original sources in archives, apparently unaware that online resources were available that could have enabled them to locate the information they were seeking in a few minutes. On the other hand, by locating specific records in sources only available in archives I have sometimes been able to overcome brick walls in a few minutes that clients had been struggling with for years or even decades. When access to original sources is required, the options available are visiting the relevant archive to carry out personal research if this is practicable, having copies made when specific records can be identified, paying someone else to carry out research, or suspending the research for the time being. This book is not intended for complete beginners but for researchers who already have some experience of genealogical research, so comprehensive descriptions of sources are not included, but specific aspects of sources that can affect the outcome of research are discussed.

Searching for information, however, is only part of the genealogical research process, as any information found must be evaluated and sound conclusions established. It is all too easy in the pre-Victorian period to assume that a record that has been found must relate to the ancestor who is the focus of research simply because the name is the same, the age is about right and they were living in the same place. People sometimes assume that their ancestor who was an agricultural labourer must have been related to the lord of the manor because they lived in the same parish and had the same surname, but such a relationship is very unlikely. Our ancestors lived in a very different world, and interpreting evidence found in historical records requires understanding not only the original purpose of those records but also the historical context in which they were created.

A major consideration in writing a book on this topic has been the issue of terminology, as many of the terms used by genealogical researchers, such as evidence, proof, source and record, are neither defined nor used consistently. More has been written on such topics in the United States, where the production of fully documented genealogical reports has assumed a greater significance. Where there is agreement about how specific terms should be used I have followed accepted practice, but otherwise I have used definitions that I consider are the most appropriate to enable concepts to be understood. Because of differing views about the circumstances in which it is appropriate to describe someone as a 'genealogist', I have used the generic term 'researcher' to refer to anyone investigating their own ancestry for their own interest.

As the number of Jews in England and Wales in the pre-Victorian period was small and the sources are specialized, there is no mention of research on Jewish ancestry in this book. I have used terms as they were used in records at the time, so refer to first names as Christian names and the birth names of married women as maiden names. Dates between 1 January and 24 March before 1752 quoted in examples have been converted to new style format.

Commercial organizations entice people to pay subscriptions to access their online records by giving the impression that genealogical research is easy, which it can be for more recent generations. Research in the pre-Victorian period, however, is both complex and challenging, and in many respects resembles academic research. Although sound genealogical research is more demanding than many people realize, it can be made slightly easier with appropriate guidance. My aim in writing this book has been to provide such guidance, and I hope that it will help you in tracing your pre-Victorian ancestors.

Chapter 1

THE CHALLENGES OF PRE-VICTORIAN RESEARCH

Genealogical research has been transformed since the millennium, with a huge amount of information now available online, which continues to grow at a rapid rate. Professional genealogists employed by television companies spend many hours locating elusive information on the ancestors of celebrities, but the resulting programmes give the impression that it is all a breeze. Online subscription services have invested millions of pounds in digitizing and indexing records, and need to draw in vast numbers of customers to recoup their costs and make a profit by enticing you to pay a subscription to 'find your ancestors'. Even relatively inexperienced researchers may be able to harvest a significant amount of 'low-hanging fruit' in the period after 1837 by using resources now available online.

Rapid progress is often possible when carrying out research on a family with an uncommon surname, or one that lived in the same village for several generations, giving the illusion that genealogical research is like assembling a model from a kit in which all the parts have either been supplied or can easily be identified and ordered, and it is simply a case of fitting them all together. Sooner or later, however, each researcher will encounter a brick wall, or unintentionally avoid it by incorrectly associating a record with an ancestor because it was the only one they could find. In the latter case they may continue with their research oblivious to any errors until they find a pedigree, devoid of sources, showing that this family, who weren't their ancestors in the first place, was descended

1

from royalty, and then gleefully add all these supposed ancestors to their family tree. This is quite common, as well as being understandable, and I made such mistakes myself as a novice researcher.

Some people give up research when their subscription expires or they have exhausted what they can easily find online, but the interest of others is kindled and they may join a local family history society, read books on family history, attend talks and classes and start visiting local archives. Having gained further experience, researchers may then return to their earlier research and prune whole branches from their family tree, after realizing that they had incorrectly answered the fundamental question: 'Does this record relate to my ancestor?'

The problem of misidentification arises largely because virtually none of the records used as sources of information in genealogical research were originally created with any anticipation of their future use for such purposes. This is not always apparent to researchers and may be of little consequence in straightforward post-1837 research, but becomes increasingly relevant when carrying out research in the pre-Victorian period.

1837: BEFORE AND AFTER

Many reforming changes took place, or were initiated, around the time of Queen Victoria's accession in 1837. Events of significance to genealogical research in the decade around 1837 include:

• The Great Reform Act of 1832, which reorganized parliamentary constituencies and broadened the franchise, the first step in its gradual extension to all adults, only finally achieved almost a century later.
• The Poor Law Amendment Act of 1834, which replaced the system of parish poor relief which had existed since Elizabethan times with a system based on Poor Law Unions and workhouses.
• The introduction of civil registration in 1837, which not only required the registration of births and deaths, but also permitted Protestant Nonconformists and Roman Catholics to marry in

their own churches and civil marriages to take place in Register Offices.
• The census taken in 1841, which was the first to record the names of all household members.

These and other changes have led to a significant difference between the sources available for genealogical research before and after 1837. There are several major complementary sources for genealogical research in the period from 1837 onwards:

• Civil registration records, in which birth records include the mother's maiden surname, and marriage records include the names of the fathers of the bride and groom, and often their ages.
• Census records, which include the abode at the time of the census, and the age of each person. Only the 1851 and later censuses recorded the exact place of birth of each person and their relationship to the head of the household.
• Church baptism records and church and cemetery burial records, which can supplement and corroborate information in civil registration birth and death records.

Sources in the pre-Victorian period are much more limited, and the above list is now reduced to the following:

• Parish and other church registers, containing baptism, marriage and burial records.
• Census records for people still alive in 1851 and living in Great Britain.

The description *parish registers* refers to registers of Church of England parishes, and other church registers, both Protestant Nonconformist and Roman Catholic, are often referred to as *non-parochial registers*. The generic term *church registers* will therefore be used in this book to refer to the registers of all denominations. The information recorded in church registers was much less than in civil registration records:

• The mother's maiden surname was not routinely recorded in baptism registers and the mother's Christian name was not always recorded before 1813.
• Marriage registers did not routinely record the ages of the bride and groom or the names of their fathers.
• Burial registers before 1813 did not routinely record age at death.

Although information from the 1841 census can often be useful, the 1851 census is more critical to solving genealogical problems because it was the first to record exact birthplace. The proportion of people still alive in 1851 diminishes with each previous generation until eventually no information on birthplace from census data is available. Some people were no longer living in Great Britain in 1851 as a result of voluntary and assisted emigration in the early Victorian period. The majority of the 160,000 people transported to Australia between 1787 and 1868 had left before 1851.

After carrying out research on one or two generations in the pre-Victorian period not only is no census information available, but the genealogical information recorded in church registers is limited and not necessarily sufficient in itself to enable relationships between people of different generations to be established with certainty. In many instances church registers could have served such a purpose for several decades after the records were made, because relevant unrecorded information could have been supplied from the personal knowledge of people who were still alive at the time, but this would have been lost when the last of those people had died, unless it had been recorded elsewhere, such as in a family bible.

The stark reality that the records used in genealogical research were rarely created in anticipation of such future use becomes increasingly apparent in the pre-Victorian period. Research now often resembles trying to construct a model from a kit in which not all the parts have been supplied, some parts look so similar that it is virtually impossible to identify the correct one, and the availability of the missing parts from other sources is uncertain.

Researchers who have already traced their ancestry back through several generations will be aware that the basic process of genealogical research for each ancestral line involves working backwards one step at a time. A single step in this process is sometimes referred to as a *genealogical question, research question* or *genealogical problem*. The word question suggests that a definite answer is likely to be possible, whereas problem implies that it may or may not be possible to find a solution. As the latter situation more accurately reflects the outcome of research in the pre-Victorian period, the term genealogical problem will be used in this book.

The two essential sources for post-1837 research are the GRO indexes and the decennial censuses, which have now been available through online subscription services for several years. Although the transcriptions of these sources and the search facilities vary from one service to another, large online subscription services such as Ancestry, Findmypast and The Genealogist are competitors in the provision of these two key resources, so researchers are often able to carry out post-1837 research reasonably effectively with a subscription to only one, supplemented by the purchase of relevant birth, death and marriage certificates. In the pre-Victorian period, continuing to use only one online subscription service may result in some 'low-hanging fruit' being found, but genealogical research in this period generally requires not only the use of a wider range of sources but a completely different approach.

The characteristics of genealogical research in the pre-Victorian period can be summarized as follows:

• The amount of genealogical information recorded in church registers is usually minimal, and not all church registers have survived.
• The solving of genealogical problems often requires additional information from sources other than church registers, and is sometimes possible using other sources even in the absence of church registers.
• The sources of information available for each individual or family are largely dependent on their social, religious and occupational background.

• It is usually necessary to use a combination of sources available online and original sources only available in archives.
• Original sources containing information relating to a particular individual or family may be located in more than one archive.
• Finding solutions to genealogical problems may require the identification and searching of very specific sources, for which search tools may not be available.
• Digitized sources and search tools available through different online search services are often complementary rather than being alternative versions of the same source.
• Knowledge of the history of the period and of the local area becomes increasingly relevant to enable information in records to be interpreted and evaluated as evidence.

This book is about genealogical research in England, but baptisms, marriages and burials of people who spent some or most of their lives in England may have taken place in other parts of the British Isles. Some people living near the Scottish and Welsh borders were born in those countries or lived there for periods of time. There is a good chance that marriages and baptisms in the pre-Victorian period can be found if they took place in Wales or Scotland, but not in Ireland, as the majority of Irish church registers were destroyed in a fire at the Public Record Office in Dublin in 1922. Although the sources for genealogical research in Wales parallel those in England, sources for research in Scotland are significantly different.

THE INADEQUACY OF CHURCH REGISTERS
Not only did church registers record less genealogical information than civil registration records, but they were not always well cared for, so some no longer survive or are very defective. Although Anglican parishes were required to keep parish registers, both their regular upkeep and subsequent preservation were often neglected. Researchers may assume that parish registers were in the care of conscientious clergymen living in vicarages next to their churches,

but that was not always the case in the pre-Victorian period, particularly in rural areas.

In the eighteenth century the profession of Church of England clergyman was more of a career than a calling, and the right to appoint the incumbent of a parish was often in the hands of one of the local gentry. Clergymen could be appointed as incumbents of more than one parish, sometimes some distance apart, a practice known as pluralism. For example, Timothy Millechamp was appointed rector of Colesbourne in Gloucestershire in 1748 and vicar of North Wootton in Norfolk in 1758, holding both positions until his death in 1780. The incumbent of a benefice or living was designated as a rector, vicar, or perpetual curate, depending on the historical right to levy tithes. A non-resident incumbent would appoint one or more curates (junior clergymen not having a living of their own) to serve those parishes in which he did not reside, who themselves might not be resident in the parishes they served, so the parish registers may have been left in the custody of the parish clerk.

A clergyman was often referred to in official records as a 'clerk in holy orders' or simply a 'clerk', but each parish also had a parish clerk, who was a local layman with a variety of paid responsibilities. Some parish clerks kept draft registers of baptisms, marriages and burials, from which parish registers were written up at intervals, and before 1813 parish registers were sometimes written up by parish clerks rather than clergymen. In the first scholarly work to be written on parish registers in England in 1829, John Southerden Burn wrote:

> The custody of parish registers having been frequently committed to ignorant parish clerks, who had no idea of their utility beyond their being occasionally the means of putting a shilling into their own pockets for furnishing extracts, and at other times being under the superintendence of an incumbent, either forgetful, careless or negligent, the result has necessarily been, that many Registers are miserably

A small church in a rural area. Not all parishes had a resident clergyman, and even when they did, the parish registers may have been neglected.

defective, some having the appearance of being kept from month to month, and year to year, yet being deficient of a great many entries; others, having a break of several years together, while a third class are written with a carelessness, amounting to little better than a total neglect of Registry (Burn, 1829, p. 39).

There were no legal requirements for Nonconformist congregations to keep their own records of baptisms and burials, and no records survive for many congregations.

Despite their recognized deficiencies, church registers are often the only or main surviving source of genealogical information for a significant proportion of the population who were neither particularly prosperous nor extremely poor. Church registers may enable some degree of *family reconstitution*, which involves examining records for a whole family in a particular locality, usually a separate parish, and attempting to construct a family tree, identifying the records relating to each individual and establishing sound relationships between family members. Successful family reconstitution based entirely on information recorded in church registers is dependent both on a high quality of record-keeping and a relatively static population and is discussed further in Chapter 11.

As outlined in the previous section, church registers recorded less genealogical information than civil registration records. The only relationship recorded explicitly in most baptism records was between the child and the father. Even when the mother's Christian name was recorded, establishing her maiden surname is usually dependent on correctly identifying her marriage to the child's father, together with any earlier marriages. Dates of baptism and burial were recorded in most church registers rather than dates of birth and death. Baptisms usually took place within the first few days or weeks after birth, but some late baptisms took place that were not identified as such in records.

The first stage of research in church registers in the pre-Victorian period often involves searching for a baptism record for a person whose place of birth, estimated year of birth and father's name have been established from post-1837 sources. It is normal practice in genealogical research to attempt to identify the baptism records for all the siblings of each direct ancestor, and also the burial records of any who died in childhood.

Having found the baptism records for an individual and their siblings, the next step is to identify the marriage record for the parents. This is not always straightforward because of the absence of the mother's maiden surname in baptism records, and can be particularly difficult in densely populated areas if the man had a common surname such as Smith or Taylor and a common Christian name such as John, William or Thomas, and the woman also had a common Christian name such as Mary, Sarah or Elizabeth. Family reconstitution may enable the date of the marriage to be estimated and corroborating evidence may be available from other sources. Searching for marriage records is generally much easier when a complete marriage index is available for the relevant area.

The first pre-1837 marriage record to be encountered often comes as a shock to researchers because it includes neither the ages of the bride and groom nor the names of their fathers. The next step is usually to search for a baptism record for the spouse whose ancestry the researcher wishes to investigate, but this requires clues to the place of birth and the approximate year of birth. Information on exact birthplace is usually only available for people who were still alive in 1851 and living in Great Britain (England, Scotland and Wales).

To calculate the approximate year of birth requires some record of age, which for people who had died before 1851 is usually their age at death. People were buried within a few days of death, so the date of a burial is always a close approximation to the date of death. Age at death was recorded from the late eighteenth century onwards in the burial registers of some dioceses and in a small number of other parishes scattered throughout the country, but 1813 is of more general significance because printed baptism and burial registers were introduced that year as a result of George Rose's Act, as explained in most introductory genealogy books. Age at death was routinely recorded in burial registers from 1813, together with abode, but there was no provision for the names of the parents of deceased children or the husbands of deceased women to be recorded as had been done previously in some parishes, although a few clergymen did record such information. Because of the minimal amount of information recorded in burial registers, both before and after 1813, it may not always be possible to associate a burial record with a specific person to a sufficiently high level of confidence.

Even when a death certificate is obtained for an adult male who died after 1837, it may not always be possible to establish that it relates to the person who is the focus of research without corroborating evidence. Death registration records for adult males did not record any genealogical information, although they did record occupation, which was not routinely recorded in burial registers. Deaths did not have to be certified by doctors until 1875, and in the earlier period of civil registration the informant was usually someone present at the death or in attendance during the last illness, not necessarily a relative. The relationship of the informant to the deceased person was also not recorded.

If the age at death of a woman was not recorded or a burial record cannot be found, it is usually possible to estimate her approximate year of birth from her childbearing history if she had a large number of children spanning a period of 20–25 years, confirming that she must have married in her late teens or early twenties. Such an estimate cannot reliably be made for men, because although husbands were often of similar age or slightly older than their wives, sometimes the age difference was considerable.

If the place of birth is unknown, the most likely places where a baptism might be expected to be found are the parishes where a person married or lived following marriage. However, since the baptism is being sought of someone whose father's name is unknown, the fact that a baptism record for a person of the same name can be found in one of these parishes around the right time does not provide sufficient evidence that it relates to the person who is the focus of research.

The search for a baptism in the most likely parishes will result in one of three outcomes:

- no baptism records
- only one baptism record
- two or more baptism records.

If no baptism records can be found in an expected location, the two possible explanations are that the person was actually born in the area but there is no surviving record of their baptism, or that they were born elsewhere. The possibility of solving genealogical problems in the absence of baptism records is usually dependent on the availability of other sources containing evidence of relationships between members of a family or of relocation from a different area.

Finding two or more baptism records for people of the same name around the same time is relatively common, not only in densely populated areas but also in relatively sparsely populated rural parishes where particular surnames were concentrated. It may be possible to eliminate one or more baptism records as possibilities by identifying distinct family groups using the technique of family reconstitution, particularly when evidence can be found that one or more individuals either died in childhood or never married. Otherwise, distinguishing between two or more people born around the same time in the same area is usually dependent on the availability of other sources containing evidence of relationships between individuals.

Only one baptism record in the relevant area for a child who does not appear to have died before reaching adulthood, however, even though it seems to fit, cannot just be assumed to relate to the person who is the focus of research without corroborating evidence, as there may be alternative explanations. In a sparsely populated parish the probability is relatively high that a baptism record and a marriage record for the same name 20–30 years apart relate to the same person, but this probability decreases as the density and mobility of the population increase. In a more populous parish it is quite possible that someone who had been born there could have left the parish and another person with the same name and of similar age could have arrived and subsequently married, giving the illusion of only one person.

In favourable circumstances, such as in a sparsely populated rural parish with well-kept parish registers, it may be possible to establish that a baptism record and a subsequent marriage record must relate to the same person by family reconstitution. When family reconstitution from church registers alone is impossible or inconclusive, establishing relationships between different generations requires finding further evidence in other sources. Sources that include information about relationships between family members, sometimes in great detail, include:

- wills
- deeds
- manorial records
- records of civil disputes in the equity courts (Chancery proceedings)
- monumental inscriptions
- settlement certificates, settlement examinations and removal orders
- bastardy documents
- educational, apprenticeship and employment records.

Some sources, including records of the criminal and ecclesiastical courts and some employment records, contain little or no genealogical information, but recorded the ages of individuals on specific dates, which can sometimes confirm a person's identity or enable two people of the same name to be distinguished. Sources such as army records and the minute books of the Boards of Customs and Excise recorded details of employment, including the locations where men served, which may enable the baptisms of children of the same parents in several different locations to be identified.

Carrying out further research on earlier generations only makes sense if sufficient weight of evidence can be found that a baptism record and a subsequent marriage record relate to the same person. In the absence of such evidence, any further research would only result in the identification of possible or probable ancestors. It is fairly common to be able to trace an ancestral line back to a parish or group of neighbouring parishes in the mid- or late eighteenth century where there is evidence that people with the same surname had been living for many previous generations. However, as a result of the minimal genealogical information in church registers and in the absence of other surviving sources it is frequently impossible to establish sound relationships between the earlier generations. When no further sources can be identified, experienced researchers will call a halt, at least for the time being, and turn their attention to a different ancestral line. Inexperienced researchers will often continue to add possible earlier generations of ancestors to their family trees because the names and dates seem to fit, but based on insufficient evidence.

The inadequacy of church registers as a source of evidence for relationships between individuals of different generations was recognized long before family history in the modern sense became popular. At a time when most genealogical research was still concerned with relatively prosperous families, many professional genealogists considered that church registers should be the last place to look. Initial research focused on sources in which relationships were recorded, such as apprenticeship and educational records, wills, manorial records and Chancery proceedings. Church records were only used for confirmation of events when relationships between the members of a family had already been established. Such an approach is still applicable in certain circumstances, but is not usually appropriate when carrying out research on the majority of the population from less prosperous backgrounds, for whom church registers are sometimes the only surviving source of genealogical information.

THE HISTORICAL CONTEXT

Genealogical research can often be carried out successfully in the period after 1837 without much knowledge of the historical context, but in the pre-Victorian period relevant historical knowledge assumes a greater importance and in some cases may be critical to the interpretation of evidence or the identification of further sources. Knowledge of the history of a particular time period, both in general and relating to a specific locality, can sometimes lead to a plausible explanation for a sequence of events that would otherwise appear improbable or inexplicable, and may enable records to be identified containing relevant evidence, as demonstrated in the following example.

Although no record of the marriage appears to have survived, it is almost certain that John Smurthwaite, baptized in the City of Durham in 1778, married Agnes Latta in mid- or late 1798, and records indicate that the couple had twelve children, all baptized between 1802 and 1823 at Durham, where John worked as a carpet weaver. The earlier baptisms took place during the period from 1798 to 1812 when more than the usual amount of information was recorded in parish registers in the Diocese of Durham. Baptism registers recorded the child's date of birth, the mother's maiden surname, and the place of birth of both parents. Agnes Smurthwaite died at Durham in 1835, aged 54, and the more detailed baptism records for the children born before 1813 are the source of her maiden name and her place of birth. Agnes Latta had been born at Irvine in Ayrshire, Scotland, where her baptism was recorded in 1781.

Baptism records indicate that Margaret, the first child of John and Agnes Smurthwaite, had been born in August 1799, but was not baptized at Durham until January 1803, several months after her sister Jane, who was born in June 1802 and baptized the following month. In the 1851 census Margaret, who remained unmarried, was recorded as having been born in Ireland. This suggests that her parents had probably married there, which would provide an explanation of why no record of the marriage could be found, as the majority of Irish parish registers were destroyed in 1922. If they had married in 1798, as seems likely, John would have been aged about 20 but Agnes would have been only 17.

The circumstances in which a young man from Durham might marry a 17-year-old Scottish girl in Ireland are likely to appear inexplicable at first sight, but finding out more about the history of the period and considering likely reasons why this couple might have been in Ireland can provide a plausible explanation. A significant number of British soldiers served in Ireland during the Irish Rebellion of 1798, so the most likely explanation is that John Smurthwaite had been in Ireland at that time because he was a soldier. It would also seem likely that he had previously been stationed in Agnes's home town of Irvine, where they had met.

It was actually possible to prove that this explanation was correct by identifying regiments that had served in Ireland at the time and searching army muster rolls and other military records held at TNA. These confirm that John Smurthwaite enlisted in the Durham Fencible Cavalry (Princess of Wales's Regiment of Light Dragoons) when it was raised in 1794 and served in Scotland for several years, where one of the six troops of the regiment was stationed at Irvine from late 1797. The Irish Rebellion broke out in May 1798 and the following month the regiment embarked for Ireland, where it remained until it was disbanded in September 1800.

It can be seen from this example that very specific knowledge is sometimes necessary to interpret evidence or identify relevant sources to enable genealogical problems to be solved. Although no records were found indicating that John Smurthwaite had ever been a soldier, examining the known facts about the family in the light of the history of the period enabled military records to be identified as a likely source. Relevant background knowledge, referred to in this book as *external knowledge*, is discussed in the next chapter.

FACTORS INFLUENCING THE OUTCOME OF RESEARCH
There are several factors affecting the outcome of genealogical research in general, and in the pre-Victorian period in particular:

• The survival of relevant sources: although some decisions have been made in the past regarding whether particular records should be preserved or destroyed, from the researcher's perspective the survival of genealogical sources is often a matter of chance or luck.
• If sources have survived, the feasibility of identifying specific records.
• The frequency of Christian names and surnames, and the extent to which distinctive Christian names were perpetuated from one generation to another.
• The social and economic status of the person or family concerned: as a general rule the more prosperous the family, the more records are likely to have been produced during each individual's lifetime and possibly survived to the present day.
• Continuity: it is usually easier to trace ancestors who remained in

the same parish, were members of the same religious denomination, or followed the same occupation for several generations.

The factors likely to influence success in genealogical research were highlighted by Sir Anthony Wagner in his classic work *English Genealogy* (Wagner, 1983). He stated that the prospects of success in genealogical research were dependent on four factors, which he defined as Record, Name, Property and Continuity. If Record is subdivided into survival of sources and the feasibility of identifying specific records, these factors correspond to the five categories listed above.

   As a general rule it is more likely to be possible to find solutions to genealogical problems for people who were sufficiently prosperous to own land or property, but detailed genealogical information on some people who were very poor has survived in Poor Law records. The outcome of genealogical research in the pre-Victorian period is dependent on the characteristics of the family or individual concerned, the survival of relevant sources and the feasibility of identifying specific records within them. Successfully identifying relevant sources, locating specific records and understanding and evaluating the information they contain is dependent on the skill of researchers.

BRICK WALLS

A brick wall is a genealogical problem for which no satisfactory solution has yet been found. Brick walls may be permanent and impossible to overcome or temporary obstacles capable in theory of being overcome eventually. Brick walls may be classified into three categories, depending on the possibility and feasibility of overcoming them:

• *Impossible* – end-of-the-line brick walls that it will never be possible to overcome because no relevant sources have survived.
• *Possible and currently feasible* – records exist to overcome brick walls that could be identified at the present time by skilled researchers.

17

• *Theoretically possible but not currently feasible* – records exist to overcome brick walls but it is impossible even for skilled researchers to identify them at the present time.

It is impossible to predict exactly which category any brick wall falls into, but it is often possible to identify those in the first category with near certainty if it can be confirmed that no relevant sources have survived.

Brick walls where an individual or family seems to appear out of nowhere are often the most intriguing, and are usually the most challenging, but researchers may be convinced that it should be possible to overcome them eventually with perseverance. Whether that is possible in practice is dependent on luck that relevant sources have survived, the feasibility of identifying relevant records at the time the research is carried out, and the skill of the researcher in doing so. It may only be possible to identify some relevant sources following the discovery of clues in others. Identifying records in very large sources may be impossible if no search tools are available. Some sources containing information that could overcome brick walls may be physically inaccessible, or accessible only with difficulty, such as record collections in private hands and those deposited in archives but not yet listed.

Some large sources that are currently unlisted may be listed in the future, so some brick walls currently in the third category may move up into the second. For example, information on the poorer members of society is often found in Poor Law records, which may survive in both parish records and Quarter Sessions records. Disputes between parishes over settlement and removal under the Poor Law, which frequently occurred in the late eighteenth and early nineteenth centuries, were adjudicated at Quarter Sessions. As well as counties, some cities and boroughs held their own Quarter Sessions, and records of disputes often exist in Quarter Sessions rolls and order books when no corresponding parish Poor Law records have survived. Quarter Sessions records for some counties and boroughs have been listed in detail, sometimes as a result of externally funded projects, but collections in other archives remain either unlisted or partially listed, and searching large unlisted collections is impracticable unless the approximate date of an event is known. Any new project to list Quarter Sessions records for the relevant area may therefore enable some brick walls to be overcome in the future, and the same principle applies to any other large source that is currently unlisted. The detailed listing of significant record collections in the future may therefore enable some brick walls to be overcome eventually.

Chapter 2

KNOWLEDGE AND SKILLS

At the end of the last chapter the skill of researchers was identified as a significant factor influencing the potential outcome of genealogical research. Learning how to be an effective genealogical researcher is quite different from training to be a chemist, historian or statistician, which usually takes place in a formal educational environment under the supervision of experienced teachers. Rather like gardening and do-it-yourself home improvements, genealogical research is often carried out alone or accompanied by other family members with similar levels of expertise, with little or no guidance or feedback from experienced practitioners. Genealogical research is one of the few leisure activities engaged in by the general public that resembles academic research, which is usually undertaken only after obtaining a first degree in the relevant subject. Few people beginning to research their family history already possess the necessary background knowledge and skills, but these can gradually be acquired through a combination of practical experience, reading books and magazines, membership of local family history societies, and attending talks and workshops.

Genealogical research superficially resembles historical research because both involve working with old documents, but finding and evaluating very specific items of genealogical information in a variety of different sources also requires some understanding of concepts such as logic and probability. This book is intended to act as a guidebook to research in the pre-Victorian period, and not only describes the basic principles of research but also highlights further knowledge and skills that committed researchers may need to acquire independently.

The competencies required in genealogical research in general and in the pre-Victorian period in particular can be grouped into four categories:

- knowledge of sources
- searching skills
- analytical and problem-solving skills
- external knowledge.

A further essential competence involves the recording of information, citation of sources and other aspects of keeping records and writing up research, which is particularly important when the intention is to publish or share the results of research with others, but this is a substantial topic in itself and is not covered in this book.

KNOWLEDGE OF SOURCES

Knowledge of the sources in which information might potentially be found is the most obvious competence in genealogical research and is superficially the most important, as reflected in the large number of books now available describing genealogical sources in general, specific types of source such as wills, church court records, Chancery proceedings and old title deeds, and sources relevant to researching ancestors with particular occupations or religious backgrounds. This book has not been written for complete beginners, so it is assumed that readers will already be familiar with the more common genealogical sources relevant to the pre-Victorian period. For readers who wish to refresh their knowledge of sources there are many books available. Cole and Titford (2003) is a good introduction, and Herber (2004) is a very comprehensive work covering a wide range of sources. Chambers (2006) and Oates (2012) focus specifically on sources in the period before 1837.

It is often possible to solve genealogical problems using very specific sources relating to people who belonged to particular religious denominations or followed certain occupations. The records in such sources sometimes include information on date and place of birth, parentage or both. Records of criminal trials rarely include much genealogical detail, but the records of the equity courts, in which family members engaged in civil disputes, can be a rich source of genealogical information. The main equity court was the Court of Chancery, so documents relating to these disputes are commonly known as Chancery proceedings.

Many guides have been published on researching people from particular backgrounds. They are generally inexpensive to purchase, and are often available for reference in archives and libraries. The SoG has published a significant number of titles in the 'My Ancestor' series. Guides to researching various categories of people who may be found in records held at TNA can be found on its website.

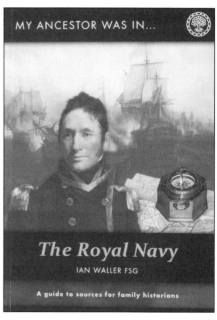

One of the titles in the 'My Ancestor' series published by the Society of Genealogists.

Sources that could potentially be relevant to carrying out research on a single ancestral line are sometimes located in two or more archives. As well as sources held in local archives, national sources such as army records and Chancery proceedings are held at TNA, and some smaller but significant sources may be held in specialist archives throughout the country. When research in specific sources is required, researchers must decide whether to attempt to carry out a search themselves or to pay to have the search undertaken by a specialist. It can take time to build up knowledge of many sources and the search tools available, so even professional genealogists sometimes engage specialist searchers to search specific sources or use the research services provided by small specialist archives to search the unique sources they hold. Specialist searchers who use sources on a regular basis are more likely to be able to find relevant records that might be missed by people who have not used them before. Although it does not provide the satisfaction of finding information as a result of personal research, engaging a specialist searcher may enable a challenging brick wall to be overcome, and can be a cost-effective option when an archive is some distance away and personal research would require expenditure on travel and accommodation.

SEARCHING SKILLS

Searching skills include establishing the location and availability of specific sources, both online and in local archives, and effectively identifying relevant records within sources. Solving genealogical problems is often dependent on finding information in new or unexpected sources, sometimes located in archives that researchers had not previously considered or known about. Searching skills therefore include understanding the nature and organization of archives and the type of sources they hold, and identifying and effectively using search tools, both computerized and traditional.

Searching skills also include a set of generic skills sometimes referred to as information skills, which are honed in certain occupations such as archive work, librarianship and other professions involving the storage and retrieval of information, and it is not uncommon for a librarian or archivist to be able to find information that has eluded less experienced searchers. In the same way that driving skills can be improved by understanding the basics of how engines, gears, clutches and brakes work, searching skills can be improved by seeking a deeper understanding of the features and nuances of a wide range of search tools.

ANALYTICAL AND PROBLEM-SOLVING SKILLS

This set of skills includes not only those that are specific to genealogical research, but also a set of generic mental skills, often referred to as critical thinking skills. Much of our thinking requires little or no effort, but critical thinking requires conscious effort. Critical thinking skills are sometimes referred to as higher-order skills, because critical thinking is more demanding than simply knowing, understanding and remembering. Although psychologists do not necessarily agree on the extent to which critical thinking skills are innate, they are gradually developed through education and refined in certain occupations. Disciplines such as mathematics, science, engineering, law and philosophy require a significant amount of critical thinking.

The possession of highly developed critical thinking skills may provide an explanation of why some people seem to have a particular flair for genealogical research. Many years' experience of genealogical research, familiarity with a wide range of sources and the ability to read old handwriting fluently do not in themselves guarantee the ability to solve difficult genealogical problems. A relatively inexperienced researcher possessing well-developed critical thinking skills may be able to overcome a brick wall that a more experienced researcher has been struggling with for years. Critical thinking skills are an integral component of research methodology in many disciplines, are generic and transferable and can be learned and improved with practice. There are many books and online courses available for readers wishing to enhance their critical thinking skills independently.

EXTERNAL KNOWLEDGE

Genealogical research involves establishing relationships between people who lived in specific places at specific times in the past, using not only information contained in records but also incorporating researchers' own knowledge about the places and times concerned. Although it has always been an implicit aspect of genealogical research, an American author, Robert Charles Anderson, has explicitly highlighted knowledge not included in sources themselves as *external knowledge* (Anderson, 2014). In this book external knowledge is discussed primarily in the context of solving genealogical problems, but it can also contribute to a deeper understanding of ancestors' lives and times, so it is also an important aspect of family history in the broader sense. It might be assumed that people with qualifications in history would have a significant advantage, but the external knowledge required in genealogical research is often quite specific and rarely covered in any depth in history courses, even at degree level.

External knowledge can be divided into two categories: *generic external knowledge* and *specific external knowledge*. Generic external knowledge is essential historical knowledge relevant to genealogical research in general. Specific external knowledge is unique to each genealogical problem and may include knowledge about the history and topography of the relevant local area and about specific identifiable characteristics of individuals and families, such as their occupation or religious persuasion.

Generic External Knowledge

The generic external knowledge required for research in the pre-Victorian period includes:

- the role of parishes and the operation of the Poor Law
- the involvement of the Church of England in non-ecclesiastical matters such as probate
- the gradual extension of religious toleration to Protestant Nonconformists and Roman Catholics and the identity of the major Nonconformist groups
- types of land tenure and the manorial system
- the civil and criminal courts
- major wars and their impact on recruitment to the army, navy and militia.

Further information on these topics can be found in books, but articles in family history magazines often describe the historical background of sources in some detail, so taking out a magazine subscription can offer an effective method of gradually building up generic external knowledge.

Unfamiliar words and concepts are likely to be encountered as research proceeds further into the past, such as 'relict', meaning a widow, 'messuage', meaning a house, and significant dates in the calendar such as 'Lady Day', 25th March. Several dictionaries of terms in genealogy and local history have been published, but since recognizing the significance of a term is often crucial to identifying the relevance of a record, it is advisable to build up knowledge of the more common terms in advance rather than waiting to encounter them. Words that have changed their meaning over time present a particular challenge, with the potential for evidence to be interpreted incorrectly, and some examples are given in later chapters. The change from the Julian to the Gregorian calendar in 1752 is described in general books on family history, so will not be explained here.

Ordinary handwriting is often fairly easy to read from the late seventeenth or early eighteenth century onwards, but earlier styles of handwriting were significantly different. Some genealogical sources, such as copies of wills in will registers and legal documents such as deeds, were written in distinctive scripts up to the nineteenth century, and may appear difficult to read at first. Many of the sources used in genealogical research were written in the expectation that they would subsequently be referred to by others (although consultation by future genealogical researchers was rarely or never anticipated), so were written with reasonable neatness, and reading old handwriting is a skill that can be learned. The study of old forms of handwriting is known as palaeography, and there are several books available, of which Marshall (2004) is particularly recommended.

Before 1733 some official and church records were written in Latin, as were later Roman Catholic records, and the occasional Latin memorial inscription, often on a tablet inside the church rather than on a gravestone in the churchyard, may be found up to the nineteenth century. Although Latin is a complex inflected language, with the exception of some adulatory memorial inscriptions written in flowery Latin by men of education who wished to demonstrate their ability to write in the classical style of Cicero or Virgil, most Latin used in genealogical sources was highly formulaic, and it is possible to learn the Latin words and expressions most likely to be

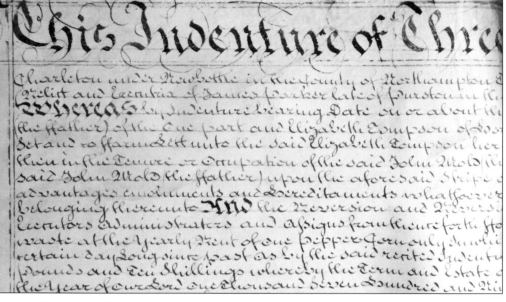

Part of a deed written in 1773. Legal documents were often written in a distinctive script, but it is possible to learn to read them with practice.

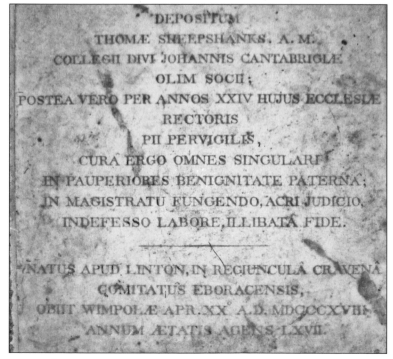

DEPOSITUM
THOMÆ SHEEPSHANKS, A.M.
COLLEGII DIVI JOHANNIS CANTABRIGIÆ
OLIM SOCII;
POSTEA VERO PER ANNOS XXIV HUJUS ECCLESIÆ
RECTORIS
PII PERVIGILIS,
CURA ERGO OMNES SINGULARI
IN PAUPERIORES BENIGNITATE PATERNA;
IN MAGISTRATU FUNGENDO, ACRI JUDICIO,
INDEFESSO LABORE, ILLIBATA FIDE.

NATUS APUD LINTON, IN REGIUNCULA CRAVENA
COMITATUS EBORACENSIS,
OBIIT WIMPOLÆ APR. XX A.D. MDCCCXVIII,
ANNUM ÆTATIS AGENS LXVII.

A memorial inscription in Latin. Latin inscriptions were often largely adulatory, but may contain information of genealogical significance. This inscription, at Wimpole in Cambridgeshire, includes the information that the Reverend Thomas Sheepshanks, who died in 1818, had been born at Linton in Craven in Yorkshire.

encountered relatively easily. Several books are available on Latin in local and family history. Some books have been written for people who wish to learn basic Latin, which requires time and effort, but others are lists of common Latin words and phrases intended for reference purposes. Classes on palaeography and basic Latin may be offered by local archives, and TNA's website includes excellent online tutorials on Palaeography, Beginners' Latin and Advanced Latin. Archivists may be able to offer limited assistance with reading old documents and some professional genealogists offer transcription and translation services.

Specific External Knowledge
Generic external knowledge is gradually acquired by all researchers over time and is cumulative. Specific external knowledge relates to specific geographical areas and identifiable characteristics of individuals and families. Although knowledge of the areas where individuals and families were living is very important, genealogical researchers are interested in the areas as they were at the time rather than as they are today. The population of many towns and cities multiplied several times over during the Victorian era, and before the nineteenth century large industrial areas were either much smaller or did not exist. In 1801 some areas that are now densely populated, such as the Teesside conurbation, still consisted of sparsely populated rural parishes.

Seaside towns grew in size following the building of railways in Victorian times, and in 1801 many areas that later became towns, such as Bournemouth and Weston-super-Mare, were very sparsely populated. Industrial towns such as Manchester, Liverpool, Leeds, Birmingham and Sheffield began to grow in the eighteenth century, but were still relatively small at the beginning of the nineteenth century. In 1801 the ten largest towns and cities in England outside London were Manchester, Liverpool, Birmingham, Bristol, Leeds, Plymouth, Norwich, Bath, Portsmouth and Sheffield, but none had more than 100,000 inhabitants. Although the population of England virtually quadrupled during the nineteenth century, some previously

Middlesbrough in 1808 and 1888. In the early nineteenth century Middlesbrough was a hamlet centred on a farmhouse, but later in the century it had been transformed into a boom town. Many of the urban areas of today were very sparsely populated before the Victorian era.

thriving towns and villages experienced absolute or relative population decline during the same period. Knowledge of the history and topography of relevant areas may enable otherwise inexplicable information to be interpreted, or provide clues to further local sources. Specific external knowledge of local areas includes:

• the location and boundaries of pre-1837 parishes
• probate jurisdictions, including the identification of any parishes that were peculiars
• families of aristocracy and gentry that owned significant amounts of land in the area, which ancestors may have rented
• manors in the area, where ancestors may have lived
• major occupations and their growth and decline
• common migration routes
• the prevalence of Nonconformity and Roman Catholicism and the location of significant congregations.

It is vital to have access to maps showing the locations of all the parishes in the area of research. The *Phillimore Atlas and Index of Parish Registers*, edited by Humphery-Smith (2003), shows pre-1832 parochial boundaries, peculiars, probate jurisdictions and the dates from which registers survive for each parish. It is often available for consultation in libraries and archive searchrooms. Relatively few new parishes were created before 1818, when the Church of England embarked on a major building programme, but additional chapels had sometimes been built at an earlier date in larger parishes or those with large populations. Chapels of ease were built as places of worship only, with all baptisms, marriages and burials taking place at the main parish church. Chapels serving specific areas within parishes and licensed to perform baptisms, marriages and burials were known as parochial chapelries, functioning in most respects as if they were parishes in their own right, and generally becoming separate parishes in the nineteenth century. Maps showing parish boundaries, such as those in the *Phillimore Atlas*, may show parishes and chapelries separately. Some areas known as *extra-parochial places*

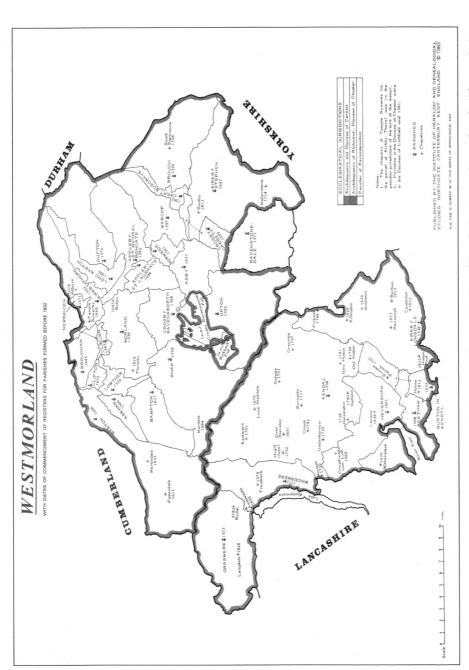

Map of Westmorland from Humphery-Smith, Phillimore Atlas and Index of Parish Registers (reproduced with permission of the Trustees and Principal of the Institute of Heraldic and Genealogical Studies, Northgate, Canterbury, www.ihgs.ac.uk)

were outside the jurisdiction of any parish, so the inhabitants did not pay church rates or poor rates, and baptisms, marriages and burials of the people living there took place in a neighbouring parish. A *peculiar* was a parish situated within the geographical boundaries of a diocese, but not under the jurisdiction of its bishop. The identification of parishes as peculiars is important because some sources, such as the wills of people who lived there, may be listed separately or be located in a different archive. Several parishes in Dorset, for example, were peculiars of the Diocese of Salisbury, so wills proved in the relevant probate courts are now held at Wiltshire and Swindon History Centre in Chippenham and not at Dorset History Centre in Dorchester.

Larger scale versions of county maps from the *Phillimore Atlas* are available for purchase from the Institute of Heraldic and Genealogical Studies (IHGS) in Canterbury, and have also been digitized by Ancestry. Other maps showing parish boundaries may be available from local archive services and family history societies.

Publications such as the *Victoria County History* include detailed information on specific parishes, and some of this information is available online. Factual information about local areas can be obtained from a variety of sources, and library local history collections, sometimes now incorporated with archives into history centres or heritage centres, are an excellent source of detailed information on specific parishes, as they often hold books and pamphlets that were produced in small quantities by local publishers and are now difficult to obtain or out of print.

Case study: external knowledge

This case study, relating to the army and militia, demonstrates how external knowledge can be used in combination with the information found in records to solve genealogical problems. It is concerned with the ancestry of Elizabeth Keen, whose baptism had been found at St Lawrence, Appleby, Westmorland (now in Cumbria), on 2 January 1766. Her father's name was recorded in

---

the baptism register as Arthur Keen, with no mother's name recorded. One sibling, George, was baptized in the same church two years earlier on 27 January 1764. These were the only baptisms for the surname Keen that could be found in Appleby.

The only burial for the surname Keen that could be found in Appleby was for Arthur Keen on 22 August 1783. Appleby was in the Diocese of Carlisle, where occupation and age were frequently recorded in burial registers in the late eighteenth century. The record of the burial included the following information: 'Arthur Keen, Pentioner, age 59'.

The description of Arthur Keen as a 'pensioner' is an important clue, because at that time the description generally referred to former soldiers and sailors in receipt of pensions.

The first stage of research involved identifying Elizabeth Keen's mother by finding her parents' marriage. Most marriages in Cumberland and Westmorland for this period can be searched online using FamilySearch, and the only marriage that could be found in the area was between Arthur Keen and Hannah Nicholson at St Cuthbert, Carlisle, on 6 December 1762. There were no clues to the origin of Arthur Keen in the marriage record, as both bride and groom were described as being 'of this parish'. Carlisle is some 35 miles away from Appleby, so although the date of marriage seems to fit with the baptism of a child just over a year later, and no baptisms of children of this couple could be found in Carlisle or its vicinity, in the absence of other evidence it cannot necessarily be assumed that these events relate to the same couple. If the mother's Christian name had been recorded as Hannah in the Appleby St Lawrence baptism register the level of confidence that these events related to the same couple would have been significantly higher.

The marriage record indicated that it had taken place by licence. Marriage bonds and allegations often recorded occupations and other clues, and although original bonds and allegations for the Diocese of Carlisle no longer survive, abstracts were made in the early twentieth century, which were subsequently published. The record of this marriage licence provides the important clue that Arthur Keen was a 'Serjeant in the Westmorland Militia'.

Relevant external knowledge relating to the militia, specifically the 'New Militia', from its formation in 1757 to the beginning of its decline in 1815, is as follows:

• The militia consisted of part-time soldiers and was only 'embodied' for home defence during periods when the country was at war and at risk of invasion. It was embodied during the Seven Years War (1756–1763) and next from 1778 to 1783 when France was allied to the United States during the American War of Independence.

• The militia was organized by county and recruited by ballot from local men, but those chosen could provide a substitute. Embodied militia regiments usually served outside the county where they had been raised.

• Militia sergeants were appointed to permanent posts, had to be able to read and write, and often had previous army experience. When the militia was not embodied, sergeants were based at the county militia headquarters.

• Since they did not serve overseas, few militiamen were awarded pensions for injury or disability while on active service, but militia sergeants, in common with regular soldiers in general, could be awarded pensions for long service on the grounds of being 'worn out'.

and specifically relating to the Westmorland Militia:

• The headquarters of the Westmorland Militia was in Appleby, the county town.

This external knowledge provides a convincing explanation of the link between the events recorded in Carlisle and Appleby: Arthur Keen married Hannah Nicholson in Carlisle in 1762 when the militia was embodied during the Seven Years War, and their children were baptized at Appleby in 1764 and 1766 when the militia was no longer embodied but Arthur Keen was a sergeant based at the militia headquarters, and he was subsequently awarded an army pension.

The next genealogical problem concerned Arthur Keen's place of birth. According to the age recorded in the burial record he would have been born about 1724, but the closest baptism that could be found in the area that is now Cumbria (Cumberland, Westmorland and the Furness area of Lancashire) is as follows:

21 April 1730 at Hawkshead, Lancashire: Arthur son of John Keen

Not only is this date several years later than expected, but Hawkshead is some 50 miles from both Carlisle and Appleby. Some parish registers from this period may be missing or defective, and as a militia sergeant who might previously have been a soldier, Arthur Keen could have been born in a different part of the country. Just because it is the only baptism record that could be found, it cannot be assumed to be correct without corroborating evidence.

From printed and online guides to researching army ancestry it can be established that registers of the award of pensions to soldiers by Chelsea Hospital from 1713 onwards are held at TNA. Pensions awarded from the late eighteenth century onwards are recorded in individual soldiers' service documents, but earlier pension awards are recorded in two series of registers containing identical information for each soldier, arranged chronologically by date of the award of pension (WO116) and by regiment (WO120). Most of the records of Chelsea Hospital of genealogical significance have now been digitized, and the records in WO120 are included in a record collection on Ancestry entitled *UK, Royal Hospital, Chelsea, Regimental Registers of Pensioners, 1713–1882*. However, the research described in this case study was carried out when WO120 was still unindexed and only available at TNA, so it was necessary to visit TNA to browse sequentially through these records on microfilm. A record in WO120/6, which lists pensions awarded to men from militia regiments, revealed the following information about Arthur Keen:

7 June 1780
Serj[ean]t Westm[orlan]d
Art[hu]r Keen, Age 50, 20 years' service. Worn out. Born at Hawkshead, Lancashire. Labourer

This confirms Arthur Keen's birthplace as being Hawkshead, and an age of 50 in 1780 corresponds to a year of birth of 1730, which is the same year as the baptism record that had been found. This indicates that the age of 59 recorded in the burial register was several years more than Arthur Keen's actual age. The reliability of recorded age at death and possible reasons for the apparent discrepancy in this particular instance are discussed in Chapter 10.

The search of WO120 was prompted by the description of Arthur Keen as a pensioner, which would not have been recorded in the burial records of most other dioceses at that time. Even if this information had not been recorded, once it had been discovered from the marriage licence record that Arthur Keen was a sergeant in the militia, and having acquired the external knowledge that sergeants were appointed to permanent posts and sometimes received pensions for long service, it would have been advisable to search these records in any case, particularly as they are now searchable online.

The external knowledge required in this case study is specific external knowledge, so it is unlikely that many researchers would already have such knowledge unless they were interested in military history or had previously carried out research on an ancestor who served in the militia. Specific external knowledge is unique to each genealogical problem, so it is usually necessary for researchers either to acquire the relevant knowledge from scratch or to enhance their existing knowledge.

Chapter 3

SOURCES

Historians generally divide sources of information into two categories according to their origin. Original or primary sources are defined as those created at the same time as or shortly after the events to which they relate, usually by people who were present when the events took place. Secondary sources are defined as those created at a later date which analyse and interpret information in original sources. They were often written by people who were not present at the relevant events, and may not have been alive at the time. These definitions lead to a simplistic distinction between original historical sources held in archives, and books and articles in academic journals written on historical topics and held in libraries. It has been recognized that this classification is not entirely satisfactory, particularly when applied to the sources used in genealogical research, in which the reliability of very specific items of recorded information is often critical. A slightly different system of classification has therefore been developed in recent years, in which sources are classified as *original sources* and *derivative sources* and separate items of recorded information as *primary information* and *secondary information*, depending on whether the person supplying or recording the information had direct knowledge of the facts or was relying on what they had heard. Original and derivative sources are discussed in this chapter, and primary and secondary information in Chapter 10.

ORIGINAL SOURCES
Organizations keep day-to-day records relating to their activities, and the effective management of records in current use is now

known as records management. After a period of time records are no longer needed for their original purpose but some may be perceived as being of enduring historical value, and are selected to be preserved. The term *archives* may be used to refer both to collections of records and to organizations such as local authority archive services and TNA, whose function is to collect, preserve and make available unique and irreplaceable records. The traditional name for local authority archives, most of which were established in the first half of the twentieth century, was *Record Office* or *County Record Office* and many still use that name. In recent years many archive services have amalgamated with library local studies collections, sometimes incorporating other heritage services such as museums and archaeology services, to form *heritage centres* or *history centres*. Some major university libraries, large public libraries, small specialist libraries and the British Library hold collections of original sources, often referred to as *manuscript collections*. Library departments holding both manuscripts and old and rare books are often referred to as *special collections*. The term *repository* or *archival repository* is sometimes used to refer to archives, but the term archives is likely to be more familiar to genealogical researchers and will be used in this book.

In an archival context the term *records* is used to describe the preserved historical records of a specific *record creator* or *originating body*. The term records is also used to describe historical records of similar type, such as parish records and army records. From the perspective of genealogical researchers, who are users of records rather than their custodians, certain record collections may be potential *sources* of information. The terms *source* and *record* are often used imprecisely and interchangeably, but the following distinction is useful in the context of genealogical research and will be used in this book:

• A *source* is a collection of records of similar type created in the past by a single organization for a specific purpose, which may now be a potential source of information in research.

• A *record* is a separate item or entry in a source, containing information relating to a specific event or person.

Original sources held in archives and used in genealogical research are found in two main physical formats:

• Bound volumes comprising multiple records, often relatively brief, each volume recording information about a large number of people or events over a period of time. Examples include church registers, other church records, probate registers, and records of education, apprenticeship, employment and membership of organizations.
• Collections of individual loose items, in which each sheet, or bundle of attached sheets, is a separate record relating to a specific event or person. Examples include original wills, grants of administration, marriage licence bonds and allegations, deeds, Chancery proceedings, settlement certificates, settlement examinations, removal orders, bastardy documents, apprenticeship indentures and military service records.

This distinction between bound volumes and physically separate items is particularly relevant when searching for information using archive catalogues, which is discussed in Chapter 9.

The term record is used slightly differently in other contexts. In computing and information retrieval a record is a discrete item in a database, and online search services such as Ancestry, Findmypast and FamilySearch use the term in this context. Although there is often a direct correspondence between a database record and an original historical record, many genealogical databases comprise index-only records in which only selected information has been extracted from historical records. Online library and archive catalogues contain catalogue records, which are database records providing descriptions of the books and archival items held by a library or archive service.

DERIVATIVE SOURCES

In recent decades the hands-on use of original sources in genealogical research has gradually diminished as record collections have been microfilmed or digitized. Routine post-1837 research does not involve the use of original sources at all, because researchers do not have direct access to the birth, death and marriage registers held by local registration services, and no longer have access to original census schedules, which are now accessible only as transcriptions or images. Many of the major sources for pre-Victorian research, such as parish registers and wills, are now routinely accessed as photographic facsimiles, in the form of microfilm copies or collections of digital images. Researchers may therefore only get the opportunity to use original sources when they need to consult more specific types of source such as deeds, family papers or Poor Law documents.

Every time an original source is copied, whether photographed or transcribed, there is a possibility of errors and omissions, and the term *derivative source* is used to describe any copy or substitute that is not the original. Mills (2015) defines derivative sources as:

> material produced by copying an original document or manipulating its content. Abstracts, compendiums, compilations, databases, extracts, transcripts, and translations are all derivatives – as are authored works such as histories, genealogies, and other monographs that are based on research in a variety of sources.

It is convenient to divide the derivative sources used in genealogical research into three categories:

• Copies that originally had the function of acting as records in their own right, and were usually made shortly after the original records had been made, such as yearly bishop's transcripts and wills copied into probate registers after being proved.
• Copies produced specifically to act as substitutes, usually many years after the originals were created and often relatively recently, with the dual purpose of making information more accessible to

researchers and preserving original sources from further wear and tear. The main types of substitute are photographic facsimiles; full transcripts; abridged and edited transcripts; and abstracts.
• Authored works such as family histories and pedigrees that include information extracted from a variety of original sources.

Copies Created as Records in Their Own Right
From the researcher's perspective, handwritten copies made from original records with the purpose of serving as records in their own right appear indistinguishable from original sources because they are of a similar age. Some sources that may appear to be original are actually copies of earlier sources that no longer survive. Although the differences between copies and originals are likely to be minimal in the majority of cases, the possibility that errors could have been made when a record was copied by hand must be taken into account when assessing the reliability of recorded information as evidence. Examples of sources that are copies of earlier sources that may or may not have survived include:

• Enumerators' books for the censuses from 1841 to 1901 are copies made by enumerators, who transcribed information from the original household schedules, which were not preserved. Some of the problems encountered when using census records undoubtedly arise because of copying errors made by enumerators.
• Sections of parish registers that have clearly been written up retrospectively. Several months or years written in the same handwriting in the same ink suggests retrospective compilation from an earlier source, which could have been written by someone else. In some cases an old parish register in poor condition may have been rewritten in its entirety decades or centuries later.
• Bishop's transcripts may have been copied directly from the parish register, but in other cases from a rough notebook. Because bishop's transcripts were required to be submitted annually, it is possible that in some parishes they were written several years before the parish register itself was written up.

• Transcriptions of original wills in will registers, or made for other purposes.

An example of significant differences between records in the parish register (PR) and bishop's transcripts (BT) can be found at Altcar, a sparsely populated Lancashire parish, in the early nineteenth century. In 1808 five baptisms were recorded, the first four of which were as follows:

23 May	Mary Daughter of Joseph the Game Keeper (PR)
	Mary Daughter of Margery Burgess (BT)
10 July	James Son to [blank] Wilson (PR)
	Alice Daughter of Mary Wilson (BT)
2 Oct	Joseph William Son of Charlotte Hunter (PR – *Charlotte* in a different hand)
	Joseph William Son of Susanna Hunter (BT)
16 Oct	John Son of James Martin (PR)
	George Son of James Martin (BT)

The handwriting in the parish register suggests that the baptism records may have been written up retrospectively, possibly after the end of 1809. Such a significant variation suggests that the parish register and bishop's transcripts could have been copied from two earlier sources, possibly separate notebooks kept by the clergyman and parish clerk. This is an extreme example of variation between a parish register and the corresponding bishop's transcripts, but it illustrates the standard of record-keeping in some parishes, which can result in some records for events that are likely to have taken place being difficult or impossible to identify.

Substitute Copies
Most parish registers are now held in archives rather than churches and they have usually been made available to users as photographic

facsimiles, initially as microfilm or microfiche, but more recently as collections of digital images, sometimes in colour. Photocopies of some original sources may also have been made. Multiple microfilm copies of some sources have been produced, and may be available for consultation in other local archives and libraries, LDS family history centres worldwide, and at the SoG in London. Some archive services have made microfilm copies of parish registers available for sale directly to researchers.

In theory, the contents of a photographic facsimile should be identical to the corresponding original source, but in practice one or more pages may have been accidentally omitted in copying, so the information in those pages will be lost to researchers unless the omission is noticed. It will be impossible to identify records in the omitted pages using indexes produced from the same photographic facsimiles. It may be possible to identify accidental omission of pages when browsing through a collection of images if specific numbered pages appear to be missing, the end of a record cannot be found on the next page, the beginning of a record cannot be found on the previous page, or there is a significant gap between the dates at the bottom of one page and the beginning of the next, although in some cases the explanation will be that the page was already missing from the original source.

Colour film was relatively expensive, so monochrome film was almost always used in microfilming, whereas most original records were written in coloured ink that may have subsequently faded on paper or parchment that has yellowed or darkened with age. Microfilming was the standard method for copying in the second half of the twentieth century, but has now been superseded by digital photography. Collections of digital images of sources such as parish registers and wills have been made available through subscription and pay-per-view online search services, by both commercial organizations and public bodies. Many of the sources had already been microfilmed, so digital images have often been produced from the existing monochrome microfilms, although some sources have been re-photographed when the microfilm images were of poor quality.

Because microfilming involved the use of photographic film, the quality of the images could not be assessed until after developing, so image quality can be extremely variable. Some sections of microfilm may be difficult or impossible to read, despite the corresponding sections of the originals being legible. If a microfilm is difficult to read it may be possible for researchers to obtain access to the original source, but this will be dependent on its condition, the archive's policy, and in some cases on the member of staff who is approached.

Some archives have made the decision to re-photograph whole record collections in colour rather than digitizing microfilms of varying quality. High-resolution digital images are sometimes easier to read than the corresponding original sources, because images can be easily magnified and software can be used to adjust brightness and contrast.

Full transcripts are exact word-for-word transcriptions of original sources, preserving the spelling, capitalization and punctuation. Transcripts may be handwritten, typed, printed or more recently made available online. Many printed volumes of transcripts were published by parish register societies in various counties from the late nineteenth century onwards. Transcripts of parish registers made many years ago by individuals may not have been published, with only a few copies made. Some typed and handwritten transcripts made before the Second World War were produced with the intention that they would be typeset and published, but this never happened, and they have subsequently been deposited in libraries and archives.

Before the widespread availability of photocopying machines in the 1970s, one or two copies of typewritten transcripts were sometimes produced using carbon paper, with one copy now available in the local archives or local studies library and sometimes another at the SoG in London. Since the 1970s many transcripts have been produced, published and sold by family history societies in the form of booklets, microfiche and CDs, and many of these transcripts can be downloaded for a modest charge from GENfair and Parish Chest.

Many transcripts have been filmed by the LDS, and the index records of baptisms and marriages for some parishes on FamilySearch have been derived from these filmed transcripts rather than from films of the original parish registers.

Most transcripts of parish registers made before the 1970s were produced from original registers still held in churches. Some recent transcripts have also been made from original parish registers held in archives, but others have been produced from microfilm copies, often by volunteers living far away from the archives holding the originals, and these may now be searchable online through services such as FreeReg. The development of the internet has also encouraged people to make transcripts they have made themselves freely available on their own websites. Transcripts made from microfilm copies may be less reliable than those made from original registers because people transcribing records from microfilm encounter the same difficulty as researchers: sections may be illegible or very difficult to read that would be legible in the original.

Transcripts may be useful when microfilms are difficult or impossible to read. Even when the corresponding sources have been digitized or are searchable online, transcripts are often much faster to browse, so can be very useful in the early stages of research to obtain an indication of the prevalence of surnames of interest, including surname variants, and to identify gaps in registers during which no events were recorded.

Transcripts in which the contents of both parish registers and bishop's transcripts have been combined and collated into a single sequence can be particularly useful, as all surviving records of baptisms, marriages and burials for a parish are then listed in one place, with any variations between the records highlighted.

The quality of transcripts varies and their accuracy is dependent on the skill of transcribers in reading old handwriting and identifying surnames and place names, as well as the extent to which the transcriptions have been subsequently checked by others. Although transcripts can be very useful in certain circumstances, original

[Oct]	10.	Elizabeth, *d.* John Dixon, Shiply.
	26.	John, *s.* Wm. Sanderson, Titlington.
Mar.	7.	Henry, *s.* Henry Reevely, Egl.
	24.	Jacob, *s.* Jacob Pyle, Cole burn.

1719.

April	5.	Eleanor, *d.* Cuthb[t] Allison, Wapperton.
	27.	Jane, *d.* Ralph Hopper, Shiply.
	16.	Ann, *d.* James Gibson, Beanly.
	16.	Elizabeth, *d.* Edward Willson, Gallalaw.
May	10.	William, *s.* William Lawson, Egl.
June	9.	Ann, *d.* John Smith, Shiply.
	13.	William, *s.* Mr. George Burrell, Bassingdon
	14.	Thomas, *s.* John Potter, O. Bewick.
	21.	Sarah, *d.* George Todd, Wapperton.
Aug.	4.	John, *s.* Peter Hume, Egl.
Sept.	6.	Mary, *d.* George Thomson, O. Bewick.
	18.	Elizabeth, *d.* Robert Allison, Beanly.
	20.	Sarah, *d.* Wm. Ellot, N. Bewick.
	20.	Thomas, *s.* Alexander Stuart, Shiply.
	22.	Camilla, *d.* Mr. Roger Pearson, Titlington.
	25.	Margaret, *d.* James Howy, Cole burn.
Dec.	20.	William, *s.* George Hall, Wapperton.
Feb.	7.	Mary, *d.* Robert Arnett, Wapperton.

1720.

April	16.	James, *s.* Wm. Thomson, Shiply.
May	17.	Ann, *d.* James Glendinnin, W. Ditchburn.
	31.	Mary, *d.* Cuthbert Collingwood, O. Bewick.
June	12.	William, *s.* William Smith, Bewick moor house.
	19.	Thomas, *s.* Thomas Moor, Shiply.
Aug.	9.	John, *s.* Mathew Mewers, Bewick Mill.
	11.	Robert, *s.* James Gibson, Beanly.
	11.	Elizabeth, *d.* Wm. Gallon, W. Lilburn.
	14.	John, *s.* Mungoe Staward, Hayrop.
Sept.	4.	Robert, *s.* Joseph Scot, Shiply.
	18.	Dorothy, *d.* John Willson, Hayrop.
Nov.	20.	Ann, *d.* William Ellot, N. Bewick.
Dec.	4.	Ann, *d.* William Gallon, Hayrop.
Jan.	17.	Peter, *s.* Peter Hume, Egl.
Mar.	17.	Mary, *d.* Anthony Strother, W. Lilburn.

1721.

·May	7.	Dorothy, *d.* Gawen Collingwood, O. Bewick.
June	4.	Mary, *d.* John Potter, O. Bewick.
	30.	Elizabeth, *d.* Robert Givare, O. Bewick.
July	16.	Ann, *d.* George Thomson, O. Bewick.
Aug.	13.	Joseph, *s.* Mr. George Burrell, Bassingdon.
Sept.	10.	John, *s.* Mathew Brown, Shiply.
	17.	Mary, *d.* Cuthbert Shell, O. Bewick.
	29.	Francis, *s.* Margaret Maine, Cole Burn.
Oct.	8.	George, *s.* Thomas Moore, Branton.

A page from a printed transcript of the parish registers of Eglingham in Northumberland, published in 1899. Transcripts can usually be browsed more quickly than handwritten original sources.

sources or photographic facsimiles of relevant records should be examined whenever possible.

Transcripts made before the Second World War are particularly valuable when the original registers were totally or partially destroyed in air raids, and when the corresponding bishop's transcripts are incomplete. Most of the parish registers of St George, East Stonehouse, Plymouth, for example, were destroyed when the church was bombed in 1941, but handwritten transcripts had previously been made, which were subsequently microfilmed and made available in local archives. These transcripts commence in 1697, whereas the bishop's transcripts only commence much later and are incomplete.

Many archives have good collections of transcripts for the area they cover. Some local studies libraries hold significant collections of transcripts, such as the local studies collection at Newcastle City Libraries which includes a large number of transcripts for parishes in Northumberland and Durham. The SoG in London has a large collection of transcripts for the whole country. Some collections of transcripts may be held in unexpected locations. Transcripts of many Cornish parish registers, for example, originally comprising part of the library of the Devon and Cornwall Record Society, are held at Devon Heritage Centre in Exeter.

Edited transcripts are transcripts that have been tidied up by correction or standardization of spelling, capitalization or punctuation. Information that is repeated in multiple records may be omitted, and other information not considered to be essential excluded, such as names of marriage witnesses. Supplementary information from other sources may have been added.

Abstracts, or summaries, of certain types of record may have been produced, particularly of wills. Wills are often lengthy and may contain a great deal of repetition and legal jargon, but the genealogical information can usually be summarized relatively concisely. It is usually much quicker to read through abstracts than original documents, so the availability of abstracts may enable relevant wills to be identified more easily. It was common practice before photocopiers became widely available in the 1970s for professional genealogists to have abstracts made of some or all of the wills for the surnames of interest in the relevant area. Some collections of will abstracts have been deposited in libraries and archives, some have been published, and others have been made available online. Abstracts made before the Second World War of wills proved in the Devon and Somerset probate courts are particularly valuable, as the original wills were destroyed in an air raid in 1942.

Authored Works

Authored works include a wide range of published and semi-published materials, including pedigrees and family histories, some produced relatively recently, but others decades or centuries ago. Although some works of this type have been published by major publishers, others have been produced in limited quantities by small publishers, individuals and local organizations. Works of this type have often been written by local historians and genealogical researchers and some may have been published with only minimal editing or checking. Although authors may have consulted an extensive range of original sources, they may have drawn unsound conclusions. The range of information collected, however, would often require a considerable amount of time and effort to compile from scratch, so such works can often be very useful, provided their limitations are recognized.

Other published works relevant to genealogical research include county histories and local histories. County histories, some published in the eighteenth and nineteenth centuries, often include historical descriptions of individual parishes. The *Victoria County History* was established in 1899 and is still in progress for many counties, although some counties are dormant, so coverage by county varies. The *Victoria County History* includes detailed historical information on the parishes in many counties, some of which is available via *British History Online*.

Local histories, relating to single parishes and towns, have been

THE

H I S T O R Y

AND

A N T I Q U I T I E S

OF THE

C O U N T Y

OF

S O M E R S E T,

COLLECTED FROM

AUTHENTICK RECORDS,

AND AN

ACTUAL SURVEY MADE BY THE LATE MR. EDMUND RACK.

ADORNED WITH

A MAP OF THE COUNTY,

And Engravings of Roman and other Reliques, Town-Seals, Baths,
Churches, and Gentlemen's Seats.

BY THE

REVEREND JOHN COLLINSON, F. A. S.

Vicar of Long-Ashton, Curate of Filton alias Whitchurch, in the County of Somerset;
and Vicar of Clanfield, in the County of Oxford.

Exutæ variant faciem per fecula gentes.　　Manilius.

IN THREE VOLUMES.
VOL. II.

BATH: PRINTED BY R. CRUTTWELL;

AND SOLD BY

C. DILLY, POULTRY; G. G. J. and J. ROBINSON, and T. LONGMAN, PATER-NOSTER-ROW;
and T. PAYNE, MEWS-GATE, LONDON;
J. FLETCHER, OXFORD; and the BOOKSELLERS of BATH, BRISTOL, &c.

MDCCXCI.

*A county history published in 1791
and a local history published in 1889.*

THE MATERIALS FOR THE
HISTORY OF THE TOWN OF
WELLINGTON, co. SOMERSET,
COLLECTED & ARRANGED
BY ARTHUR L. HUMPHREYS.

London: HENRY GRAY, 47 LEICESTER SQUARE.
Wellington: TOZER & GREGORY, SOUTH STREET.
MDCCCLXXXIX.

published since the nineteenth century. They include similar information to county histories, but are often based on a wider range of original sources. Older county and local histories sometimes include information transcribed from sources that no longer survive, or include monumental inscriptions that no longer exist or are now illegible.

Some older published works, now out of copyright, have been digitized and are available through various websites, including *Google Books* and the *Internet Archive*. In most cases the searchable content has been produced using optical character recognition (OCR). Although this is not infallible, the amount of information now available is vast. More reliable search results are obtained when searching sources that have been re-keyed from scratch, such as *British History Online*, which contains transcriptions of sources of interest to British historians, some of which may be relevant in genealogical research, such as county histories, lists of clergy and state papers.

SURVIVAL OF ORIGINAL SOURCES

Until well into the twentieth century, decisions regarding the care, preservation and intentional destruction of collections of old records rarely took into consideration their potential value as sources for genealogical research, and researchers frequently encounter brick walls that could have been overcome if sources had survived. Space is taken up storing collections of old records, and paper shortages, particularly during the two world wars, led to the collection of waste paper and the pulping of historical records whose significance for posterity was not recognized at the time. Even as recently as 1961, when the 1841 and 1851 censuses had been available for public use for some time, there was a suggestion that the 1861 census schedules, which had remained closed for 100 years, should be pulped.

As well as deliberate destruction, sources may have been destroyed by fire, flood, damp or vermin, or simply crumbled away. The parish registers of Thorverton in Devon were severely damaged by flooding when the river burst its banks in 1823, and the baptism register for Feock in Cornwall for 1813–1843 was destroyed when the old vicarage was burnt down in 1896. As recently as 1964 the parish registers of Shepton Montague in Somerset were badly damaged by a fire at the church. These are examples where the fate of the registers is known, but many other registers have disappeared without trace. In 1841, for example, it was noted that the parish registers of Tanfield in Co. Durham commenced in 1577, but fifty years later that those before 1719 had been lost. The survival of bishop's transcripts also varies considerably from one diocese to another.

Great Britain has not been invaded since 1066, but there have been periods of internal disruption. Many earlier records were lost and record-keeping was disrupted during the Civil War and Commonwealth period from 1642 to 1660. Following the restoration

Exeter following the Blitz of 1942. Some genealogical sources were destroyed during the Second World War as a result of enemy action, including wills proved in the Dioceses of Exeter and Bath and Wells held at the Exeter Probate Registry.

of the monarchy in 1660 the puritan clergy of many parishes were ejected and replaced. Although parish registers were introduced in England in 1538, many survive only from the 1660s or later. Some bishop's transcripts survive from the early seventeenth century, but they were not produced during the period from 1649 to 1660 when bishops did not exist.

Air raids during the Second World War caused the destruction of some important records, including parish registers in churches not only in cities such as London, Bristol, Coventry and Plymouth, but also a few churches in rural areas hit by stray bombs, such as Clyst St George in Devon. Other sources destroyed in air raids include all pre-1858 wills for the counties of Somerset and Devon then held at the District Probate Registry in Exeter, pre-1834 Poor Law material for the cities of Exeter and Bristol, and numerous sources that were located in London, including many army service records and the records of Trinity House and some livery companies.

Chapter 4

NAMES

The probability of being able to find solutions to genealogical problems increases when carrying out research on families with uncommon surnames and individuals with uncommon Christian names, as the number of people living at the same time who could potentially have the same name is correspondingly reduced. The repetition of distinctive Christian names in the same family from generation to generation, often following specific patterns, may also enable families with the same surname to be distinguished and family units to be reconstituted. The significance of names and naming patterns in genealogical research is discussed in this chapter. Searching for names is not always straightforward because of lack of standardization in the spelling of surnames and the recording of Christian names. Searching for name variants using search tools and archive catalogues is discussed in Chapters 8 and 9.

SURNAMES

The probability of being able to solve genealogical problems is influenced by the frequency of the surname that is the focus of research, but in the area where the family lived rather than the country as a whole. The surnames Vile, Gaylard and Hebditch, for example, are relatively rare nationally, but were very common in a small number of Somerset parishes. As a general rule, the probability of being able to solve a genealogical problem increases as the frequency of the surname in the area decreases, and vice versa.

Inexperienced researchers sometimes assume that a record they have found could not possibly relate to their ancestor because the spelling of the surname was different from that used by later generations, but the spelling of surnames in the pre-Victorian period was inconsistent. The names of people who could not write their own names were often recorded according to how they sounded to people recording the information. It was not uncommon for clergymen to have previously lived in different parts of the country, so they were not necessarily familiar with either local surnames or local accents.

Surnames evolved as descriptions to distinguish people with the same Christian name, and by the late Middle Ages had become fixed and hereditary in England. Surnames can be divided into several categories:

• surnames based on relationship, usually between child and father, known as patronymic surnames, such as Johnson and Wilson
• occupational surnames, such as Wright and Fuller
• locative surnames, derived from specific place names, such as Dent and Blakeney
• topographical surnames, derived from geographical features, such as Broadwood and Haythornthwaite
• surnames derived from nicknames, based on physical appearance or other distinctive characteristics, such as Redhead and Sheepshanks.

Some surnames derived from place names can be traced to several different locations. The surname Bradford could be derived from places of that name in several counties, including Yorkshire, Wiltshire, Somerset and Devon. Other surnames are derived from only one specific place, and were usually heavily concentrated in the surrounding area before the nineteenth century. The surname Ilderton, for example, is derived from the place of that name in Northumberland, and until the early nineteenth century was found almost exclusively in Northumberland and the northern part of Co. Durham. The sudden appearance of a distinctive locative surname in a new area is not necessarily an indication of direct migration from its area of origin, however.

Surnames based on physical characteristics were also sometimes concentrated in specific parishes. Maria Sheepshanks was born at Wisbech in Cambridgeshire in 1792, where her father, Thomas Sheepshanks, was a clergyman, but no earlier references to the surname could be found in the area. Many clergymen took up livings far away from their place of birth, but establishing the origins of Anglican clergymen is usually relatively straightforward as most had been educated at Oxford or Cambridge and lists of alumni have been published based on information in university records. It was found that Thomas Sheepshanks was the son of Richard Sheepshanks, a yeoman farmer of Linton in the West Riding of Yorkshire, where many earlier generations of people with the surname can be found.

Population increase and low levels of mobility caused some surnames to become concentrated in particular parishes. The migration of an individual, couple or family to a new area in which the surname had not previously occurred often resulted in the gradual increase in concentration of the surname in the destination area over several generations. It is not unusual to find that everyone born in a parish with a particular surname was descended from one identifiable ancestor. There were several families with the surname Brotherton living in Berwick-upon-Tweed in Northumberland in the nineteenth century, all of whom were descended from John Brotherton, an out-pensioner of Chelsea Hospital who died there in 1807. Soldiers were awarded pensions for injury or long service, but during times of war pensioners of all ages who were still capable of using a musket were liable to be called up for garrison duty in 'invalid' companies to release regular soldiers for service elsewhere. Berwick was a garrison town, and it seems likely that John Brotherton had been sent there in the period 1778 to 1783 when Britain was at war with France. In any event, he settled in the town, married a much younger woman, and four children were baptized there in the period from 1786 to 1792. Before the nineteenth century the surname Brotherton was concentrated in Yorkshire and Lancashire, but was uncommon in Northumberland. Three men named John Brotherton in the relevant age range are listed in the pension records of Chelsea Hospital. One had been born in Yorkshire, one in Lancashire and one in Staffordshire. It seems almost certain that the John Brotherton who settled in Berwick was one of these three men, but no evidence has yet been found to indicate which.

Change of surname among the lower and middle classes was rare, although spelling sometimes changed gradually over time. Among the landed gentry, a man dying without direct male descendants would sometimes choose another relation as his heir on condition that he assumed the surname. Ralph Edge of Strelley, Nottinghamshire, died without issue in 1684, and named his first cousin once removed, Richard Conway of Marston Montgomery, Derbyshire, as his heir, who subsequently took the surname Edge. Richard Edge's son, another Ralph Edge, who died in 1766, also had no direct male-line descendants, and his grandson Thomas Webb became his heir, and took the name Thomas Webb Edge.

Illegitimate children, generally referred to in the pre-Victorian period as bastards, were usually baptized with their mother's surname, and establishing their father's identity may not be possible. The father's name was occasionally recorded in baptism registers, and sometimes in Poor Law records. Further information on researching bastards can be found in Paley (2011). Illegitimate children who were acknowledged by their fathers sometimes took their father's surname and were often referred to in wills and other legal documents as 'natural children' rather than bastards. The will of John Castle, a London tobacconist who had been born in the North Riding of Yorkshire in 1717, was proved at the Prerogative Court of Canterbury in 1786. He died childless and left several legacies to nephews and nieces in Yorkshire, including one to 'my nephew John Tweddle, natural son of my sister Mary Castle'.

CHRISTIAN NAMES

During the hundred years from 1750 to 1850, a period of relatively high mobility in which the population more than doubled, not only was the range of Christian names in common use relatively limited but the practice of giving middle names to children in lower-class families only became common towards the end of the period. During this period around half of girls were named Mary, Elizabeth, Sarah or Ann and almost half of boys were named William, John or Thomas. Less common Christian names such as Alexander, Caleb, Ebenezer, Josephine, Louisa and Priscilla are likely to enable specific individuals or families to be identified more easily, particularly if such names were perpetuated from one generation to another.

There was considerable variation in the popularity of Christian names between different parts of the country, and even from parish to parish, so some names were more common in specific localities than might be expected. Some biblical names of Old Testament origin, such as Moses, that were relatively uncommon in the country as a whole, were quite common in some areas and particularly in some Nonconformist congregations. Between 1750 and 1850 some diminutive names for girls, such as Betty, short for Elizabeth, Fanny, short for Frances, and Jenny, short for Jane, were given as baptismal names. This practice seems to have applied mainly to girls' names, and although many men were known as Jack, they had usually been baptized as John.

Because of the limited number of Christian names in common use, the probability of a widower marrying a woman with the same Christian name as his first wife is higher than might be expected. James Edgell married Sarah Parsons in 1757 in Bristol, and five children were born in the period 1758 to 1767. Sarah died in 1769, and six months after her death James Edgell remarried, to another Sarah, a widow named Sarah Witchell. Examples can even be found of men marrying two women with exactly the same name. James Davenport, Vicar of Stratford-upon-Avon, married a spinster named Margaret Webb in 1791. She died in 1796 and he remarried in 1808 to another Margaret Webb, who was the widow of his first wife's cousin.

An uncommon Christian name can reduce the probability that there were two or more people with the same name living in the same area. Adherence to naming patterns was common in the pre-Victorian period, with the result that Christian names from both a paternal and a maternal line were sometimes perpetuated over many subsequent generations. The extent to which naming patterns were followed and rigidly adhered to varied from area to area and from family to family, but a typical pattern for sons would be:

• first son named after the paternal grandfather
• second son named after the maternal grandfather
• third son named after the father
• subsequent sons named after paternal then maternal uncles.

Naming patterns for daughters often followed a similar pattern, but sometimes with the names of the mother's relations taking precedence. Children were usually named after close relatives but sometimes after family friends who acted as godparents, which could introduce a new Christian name that had not previously been a family name.

If a child died in infancy or early childhood it was common practice for the next child of the same sex to be born to be given the same Christian name. This may seem somewhat macabre today, but the purpose was to ensure that a Christian name of family significance was perpetuated rather than to commemorate a child who had died. In the sixteenth century and earlier it was not uncommon for two living children of the same parents to be given the same Christian name, who would be distinguished as 'the elder' and 'the younger', but this practice had virtually died out by the seventeenth century. Siblings were sometimes given names that would today be regarded as variants or alternatives, and examples can be found of sisters named Maria (which may have been pronounced Mar-EYE-ah) and Mary, and Elizabeth and Eliza, and of brothers named John and Jonathan.

Adherence to naming patterns was stronger in some areas than others. In some families the origin of all the Christian names of siblings can be inferred from the names of close relatives. Thomas Emmerson married Dorothy Jolley in 1807 in Tanfield in Co. Durham and they had the following children, with the most likely origins of their Christian names shown:

George (1807–1814)	paternal grandfather
Margaret (1809–1814)	maternal grandmother
Thomas Jolley (1812–)	maternal grandfather (and mother's eldest brother)
George (1814–)	paternal grandfather
John (1816–)	father's only brother
Margaret Ann (1818–)	maternal and paternal grandmothers
James (1820–)	mother's second eldest brother
Ralph (1822–)	mother's third eldest brother
William (1824–)	father's uncle
Dorothy Jane (1828–)	mother and mother's sister

Naming patterns can be both a help and a hindrance in genealogical research. The use and perpetuation of distinctive Christian names can help to reduce ambiguity. On the other hand, the proliferation and perpetuation of common Christian names often resulted in several people of similar age with the same name living in the same area at the same time.

Children were often named after their grandparents, and it was fairly common for two or more children of the same name and with the same grandparents to be born around the same time. If cousins of the same name were born several years apart, it may be possible to distinguish between them fairly easily if their age at death can be established, as in the following example, where three cousins named John Thompson were born in 1793, 1803 and 1814.

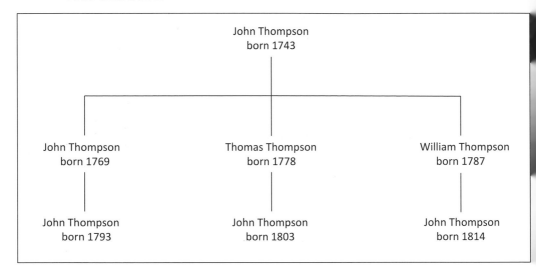

In some cases, cousins of the same name were born relatively close together, as in the following example, where three cousins named William Hunter were born in the period 1798 to 1803:

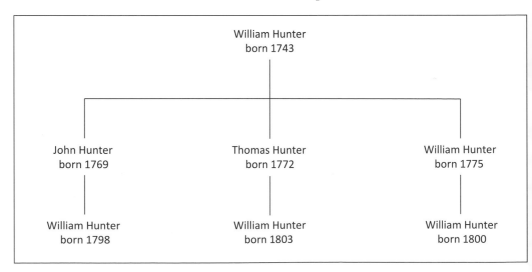

Even if the parish had a small and stable population and there can be no doubt that everyone baptized with the same surname must have been descended from one male ancestor, it is not always possible to fit people into family groups with certainty if children with the same name were baptized around the same time. Recorded age at death and in the censuses was not always accurate, so in this example there are three possible baptisms that could correspond to an ancestor named William Hunter born about 1800. It may be possible to reduce the number of possible candidates if it can be established that one or more children did not survive to adulthood, but this is only possible if sufficient information was recorded in the burial register, or can be found in a recorded monumental inscription or other source, to enable the identity of a deceased child to be established with certainty. Further unravelling of family relationships often requires accumulating information from a variety of sources, such as wills or Poor Law documents, depending on the social status of the family. When this is impossible, it can sometimes be determined that the father of an ancestor was almost certainly one of two or three brothers, as in the above example, so the identity of the paternal grandparents can be established, leading to the possibility of investigating earlier generations. However, as the identity of the father cannot be established, the identity of the mother is uncertain, so it is impossible to carry out further research on the maternal line.

Surnames were sometimes given as Christian names in families of all classes, and the use of such distinctive names can often enable the relationship between successive generations to be established. Giving the mother's maiden surname to a son as a Christian name was particularly common in the coal-mining areas of Northumberland and Durham. George Henderson married Eleanor Roseby in 1747, and they named their son, born in 1748, Roseby Henderson. The Christian name Roseby was perpetuated through several subsequent generations as shown below, and Roseby continued to be given as a Christian name throughout the nineteenth century.

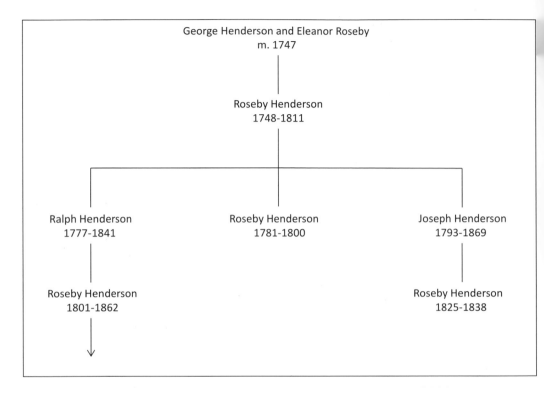

The perpetuation of an uncommon Christian name through several generations of a family may enable the various family units to be reconstituted. The families in the above example were involved in coal mining, and regularly moved from parish to parish in the Northumberland and Durham coalfield. Family reconstitution of several generations was possible because of the distinctive Christian name Roseby, but would have been difficult or impossible if more common Christian names had been given.

The practice of giving children more than one Christian name started to become common in middle-class families in the late eighteenth century. Thomas Wilkins married Mary Haighton in London in 1783, and they had nine children:

Mary Haighton Wilkins (born 1785)
Thomas Wilkins (born 1786)
Richard Haighton Wilkins (1788–1789)
Richard Wilkins (born 1789)
John Wilkins (1791–1793)
Susannah Haighton Wilkins (born 1795)
Temperance Wilkins (born 1797)
Grace Haighton Wilkins (born 1801)
Ann Wilkins (born 1803)

It was already known that Thomas Wilkins had been born at Brackley in Northamptonshire, but no baptism record could be found for Mary Haighton in either Brackley or London. It seemed likely that the couple's second son, Richard Haighton Wilkins, had been named after a family member, possibly Mary Haighton's father. It was found that several wills had been proved at the Prerogative Court of Canterbury in the early nineteenth century for men named Richard Haighton. The will of Richard Haighton of Longstow, Cambridgeshire, who died in 1810, revealed that he was Mary Haighton's uncle, a clergyman who was a childless widower, and the will of Richard Haighton of Toft, Cambridgeshire, who died in 1812, that he was Mary Haighton's brother. Richard Haighton the clergyman had been educated at the University of Cambridge, and alumni lists indicate that he had been born at Baildon in Yorkshire in 1735, the son of another clergyman also named Richard Haighton. The baptism of Mary Haighton was found at Baildon in 1760, daughter of Thomas and Susannah Haighton, together with the baptism of her brother Richard in 1758. The amount of work required to identify Mary Haighton's parents was minimized by identifying the Christian names of likely testators based on the names given to children in later generations.

Middle names were sometimes given to illegitimate children, and can provide a clue to the father's name. If the illegitimate son of Hannah Drake was named William Criddle Drake, it is very likely that his father's name was William Criddle, but this should not be assumed, as other explanations are possible.

The practice of giving children two or more Christian names became more common in families of all social classes in the Victorian period, with the names given often relating to other family members, sometimes long since deceased. Alexander Brotherton, a rope maker, married Agnes Smurthwaite in Berwick-upon-Tweed in Northumberland in 1867 and their first six children were named as follows:

Margaret Ann Snowdon Brotherton (1867–1869)
James Gilbert Snowdon Brotherton (born 1869)
Margaret Ann Snowdon Brotherton (born 1871)
Agnes Latta Brotherton (born 1875)
Robina Cowe Brotherton (born 1877)
Charles George Smurthwaite Brotherton (born 1879)

James was the name of Alexander's father, and Ann was the name of his stepmother. Charles George Smurthwaite was the name of Agnes's father, and Margaret Snowdon her mother's maiden name. Robina Cowe was the maiden name of Agnes's sister-in-law, the wife of her brother James Smurthwaite. The two names of significance to the pre-Victorian period are Gilbert Snowdon (1778–1861), Agnes's maternal grandfather, and Agnes Latta (1781–1835), the maiden name of Agnes's paternal grandmother. Agnes Latta Brotherton, born in 1875, was therefore named after her great-grandmother Agnes Latta, who had died forty years before she was born. Although naming a child after a long-deceased great-grandparent was not particularly common, the names given to children in the Victorian period can sometimes provide clues to the names of earlier ancestors or corroborate evidence that has already been found.

Abbreviations of Christian names are commonly found in all sources used in genealogical research. *Abbreviation* in the strict sense refers to a word that has been shortened by dropping the ending, and a word in which some of the middle letters have been omitted but the final letter is still present is referred to as a *contraction*. Tho: is an abbreviation of Thomas and Thos or Tho[s] a contraction. The omission of letters in abbreviations was often denoted by a colon, for example Tho: for Thomas, Hen: for Henry and Nich: for Nicholas. The final letter of a contraction was often written as a superscript, so Jos[h] would be an abbreviation for Joseph, or possibly Josiah, but never Joshua, for which Josh: would be used. Other common contractions are Marg[t] for Margaret, W[m] for William, H[y] for Henry, and Eliz[th] for Elizabeth. Jno or Jn[o] was short for John, and never for Jonathan. This abbreviation was used for several centuries, but there seems to be no satisfactory explanation of its origin.

CHRISTIAN NAMES RECORDED IN LATIN

Names in parish registers were sometimes recorded in Latin before 1733, as were names in Roman Catholic registers from the 1780s onwards. Latin is a complex inflected language, with the endings of words changing according to the meaning, but most Latin found in genealogical sources is highly formulaic. Surnames were not usually translated, but Christian names were routinely translated into their corresponding Latin form, with the endings, known as case endings, changing according to the grammatical significance of the word. The following section is intended to provide a very basic introduction to enable names recorded in Latin to be identified.

A typical Latin baptism record is likely to be in the form:

Johannes   filius   Johannis   Hodges   baptizatus   fuit

There is no separate word for 'of' in Latin, so the literal word-for-word translation of the above is:

John   son   of-John   Hodges   baptized   was

Johannes is the nominative case (the simple name) and Johannis the genitive case (meaning of-John). *Filius* means son and *filia* means daughter. Sometimes *fuit* was replaced by *est* (*est* was correct classical Latin but *fuit* was used in medieval Latin). *Baptizatus fuit* (or *baptizatus est*) was used to record the baptism of a son and *baptizata fuit* (or *baptizata est*) the baptism of a daughter.

65

It is important to be aware that the meaning of a Latin sentence is not determined by its word order as in English but by the case endings. A Latin record may be translated incorrectly if case endings are ignored and it is assumed that English word order has been used. The literal word-for-word translation of the Latin:

Johannis   Hodges   filius   Robertus   baptizatus   fuit

is:

of-John   Hodges   son   Robert   baptized   was

so the correct English translation is:

Robert son of John Hodges was baptized

Contractions of the Latin forms of Christian names sometimes appear in original records, such as Johannes shortened to Johes and Johannis to Johis, with the omission of letters shown by a straight or wavy horizontal line. In computerized indexes Latin Christian names have often been simply transcribed as they stand. In a baptism record such as:

Jana filia *Johis* et *Aliciae* Robinson baptizata fuit

the names of the parents are likely to have been indexed as *Johis* and *Aliciae*. Correctly establishing that the father's name was John is dependent on recognizing Johis as an abbreviated form of Johannis, the genitive form of Johannes, which is the Latin form of John.

The Latin words used in marriage records were much more variable, but because the names of two people of the opposite sex were recorded, there is less scope for ambiguity. Burial records are generally straightforward and usually include the words *sepultus est* (*fuit*) or *sepulta est* (*fuit*).

It is advisable to become familiar with the Latin forms of the most common Christian names before encountering them for the first time. Many are fairly obvious (the genitive *of* form is shown in brackets):

Edward	Edwardus (Edwardi)
Henry	Henricus (Henrici)
John	Johannes (Johannis)
Richard	Ric(h)ardus (Ric(h)ardi)
Robert	Robertus (Roberti)
Thomas	Thomas (Thomae)
Mary	Maria (Mariae)
Agnes	Agnes or Agneta (Agnetis)
Ann	Anna (Annae)
Alice	Alicia (Aliciae)
Elizabeth	Elizabetha (Elizabethae)
Jane	Jana (Janae)

The following names are not quite so obvious:

Charles	Carolus (Caroli)
James	Jacobus (Jacobi) – also used for Jacob
Giles	Egidius (Egidi or Egidii)
Geoffrey	Galfridus (Galfridi)
Hugh	Hugo (Hugonis)
Lewis	Ludovicus (Ludovici)
Ralph	Radulphus (Radulphi)
Joyce	Jocasta (Jocastae)

Some names were recorded in several different Latin forms, including:

Christopher	Christophorus (Christophori) or Xtopherus (Xtopheri)
Walter	Walterus (Walteri) or Gualterius (Gualteri)
William	Willelmus (Willelmi) or Gulielmus (Gulielmi) or Guglielmus (Guglielmi)

The genitive ending *ae* was sometimes written as *æ* or *e*, so Aliciae may appear as Aliciæ or Alicie.

Before the mid-eighteenth century it was rare for children to be given the Latin forms of Christian names, such as Maria, Anna and Joanna, as names in their own right. When recorded in Latin in pre-1733 parish registers, Maria, Anna and Joanna/Johanna should normally be translated as Mary, Ann(e) and Joan. The Latin form Jacobus is ambiguous, as it was used for both Jacob and James. Although James was generally more common than Jacob in the period before 1733, the name Jacob did occur, and it is not always possible to establish whether the name was actually James or Jacob from a single record in a parish register.

Chapter 5

SOCIAL STATUS

In the twentieth century, and particularly in the decades following the Second World War, educational and employment opportunities made it possible for people from relatively poor backgrounds to become upwardly mobile, and in some cases to achieve positions of considerable power, prestige and wealth. Such social mobility in the pre-Victorian period was very rare, as the position of people in society was dependent on the circumstances of their birth and not their abilities or talents, so virtually everyone remained in the social class into which they had been born.

During the Middle Ages creation was believed to consist of a Great Chain of Being from God at the highest point to inanimate matter at the lowest, and human beings were part of this chain, with the ranks of society descending in a hierarchy from the king at the top to serfs at the bottom. Although social rank gradually became less rigid after the Middle Ages, the belief that each person was born into their station in life persisted, at least among people in positions of power, until relatively recent times. Social mobility began to increase in the late eighteenth century with the growth of the middle class, which grew in size and importance in the Victorian period, and people started to be defined by their occupation rather than the circumstances of their birth.

The relative constancy of social status in the pre-Victorian period is relevant to genealogical research for several reasons. Firstly, it provides an indication of how far back it might be possible to research an ancestral line. Secondly, external knowledge concerning social status can enable information in records to be interpreted correctly. Awareness that in the early eighteenth century 'Mr' was not a universal title for adult males but an indication of social status unlikely to be used for a labourer may enable researchers to distinguish between families with the same surname and to eliminate certain records as relating to their ancestors. Thirdly, the social status of a family is relevant to the selection of the most appropriate sources to search. For example, it would be ludicrous to start research on the ancestry of an illiterate agricultural labourer by looking at wills for the same surname proved at the Prerogative Court of Canterbury.

The social status, education and occupation of an individual or family are of considerable significance to the outcome of genealogical research. In general, the quantity of records generated during a person's lifetime was related to their level of prosperity, reflected in their social status, although significant quantities of records were also produced under the Poor Law for some people who were very poor. The survival of records is dependent both on their perceived importance and subsequent chance events. Wills have been routinely preserved because of their relevance to the descent of land and property and their potential importance in resolving disputes many years later. Furthermore, their value as a genealogical source has long been recognized by the more prosperous classes, who until relatively recently were the only people in a position to engage in genealogical research. Poor Law records, on the other hand, were not generally perceived as being of any lasting interest, other than to a few local historians, some of whom rescued them for posterity. The stigma of the Victorian workhouse, which persisted for several decades into the twentieth century, together with salvage drives resulting from paper shortages during the two world wars, undoubtedly resulted in the destruction of many Poor Law records before their value as sources of genealogical information had been widely recognized.

In the pre-Victorian period, as today, social observers recognized three broad social categories: the upper, middle and lower classes.

These three categories, in a historical context, are also relevant to both the approach to genealogical research and its potential outcome. The *upper class* or landed elite consisted of the aristocracy and titled gentry, who owned large country estates that provided them with an income from renting land to tenants. There is little mention of the upper class in this book from a genealogical perspective because the surviving records are usually extensive and pedigrees have often been maintained for many generations. However, the detailed records kept by landowning families often contain genealogical information about people further down the social scale.

The *middle class*, sometimes referred to in the pre-Victorian period as people of the middling sort or the middling orders, incorporated a wide range of people who did not engage in manual labour, were usually reasonably well educated, and often owned some property. The middle class included families of untitled minor gentry, yeoman farmers who owned their own land, tenant farmers who rented large acreages, clergymen, lawyers, physicians, surgeons, apothecaries, Customs and Excise officers, officers in the army and navy, merchants and master craftsmen. Men from this background frequently left wills, as did many spinsters and widows, and when they did not it was usually necessary for their next of kin to obtain letters of administration. People from such a background frequently owned land, but the survival of historical records relating to the ownership and occupation of land is very variable: there are surviving deeds in profusion for some families but there is little or nothing for others. Boys from middle-class families often attended local grammar schools or minor public schools and some attended university or trained as lawyers. Others took up apprenticeships in the more prestigious crafts or joined the family business.

It is frequently possible to trace the ancestry of middle-class families back to the seventeenth century and earlier. Brick walls may sometimes be encountered in the eighteenth century for a variety of reasons, including a period of residence abroad, a preponderance of grants of administration rather than more genealogically rich wills, and destruction of relevant records. Tracing middle-class ancestry in Devon and Somerset is more difficult than in other counties because of the destruction of probate records in an air raid during the Second World War.

The marriages of people from middle-class backgrounds often took place by licence, which was more costly. A marriage licence was obtained by the applicant, usually the groom, paying a fee and signing an allegation and a bond. The allegation was a document in which the couple, or often just the groom, alleged that there was no impediment to the marriage, and the bond was a pledge to pay a significant sum of money if the allegation proved to be untrue. Further information on marriage bonds and allegations can be found in books describing genealogical sources.

Although prosperity had some influence on general health and therefore lifespan, neither the causes of diseases nor the environmental factors leading to their spread were understood and few effective treatments were available, so death in childhood and early adulthood was not uncommon in middle- and upper-class families, particularly in towns and cities.

The *lower class* consisted of families of tradesmen such as blacksmiths, carpenters, masons, wheelwrights, coopers, tailors, spinners, weavers, butchers, bakers and shoemakers, together with small farmers, small shopkeepers and innkeepers, agricultural and industrial labourers, miners, soldiers, sailors, indoor domestic servants, gardeners, grooms, coachmen and carriers. Women were involved in a variety of paid and unpaid work, with many working as domestic servants. People from lower-class backgrounds rarely owned land, but some had possessions or savings of sufficient value to justify making wills. With the exception of soldiers and sailors who sometimes married by licence because the calling of banns would have been impracticable, most people married after banns because it was cheaper.

It is not uncommon to encounter a brick wall in the mid- or late eighteenth century for people from lower-class backgrounds because of lack of surviving records, and in a few cases in the early nineteenth century for the same reason. On the other hand, if a family lived in the same parish for generations, and the parish registers were well kept, it may be possible to trace an ancestral line back to the seventeenth century.

The lower class consisted of a spectrum of levels of prosperity ranging from paupers to those who were borderline middle class, with skilled tradesmen being more prosperous than unskilled labourers, but further subdivision is not necessarily useful from a genealogical perspective because circumstances could change both within one person's lifetime and from one generation to the next, as well as varying between siblings. Examples can be found of men who, together with their wives and young children, were the subject of removal orders, but had become sufficiently prosperous to leave wills when they died several decades later. Prosperity increased in a continuum from the very poor to the extremely wealthy, so although a classification into upper, middle or lower classes is applicable to the majority of families, some hovered on the borderline between classes for several generations.

Inheritance of land and property, at a time when families were large but average life expectancy was much lower than today, had a significant impact on people's economic circumstances and has a consequential impact on genealogical research. At a time when land usually passed to the eldest son as heir, the early death of a childless elder brother could result in an unexpected improvement in the economic circumstances of a younger brother. A larger proportion of people than today never married and some who did died without any surviving children, so nephews and nieces sometimes received legacies from childless uncles or aunts. Unmarried people did not have to bear the costs of raising children and some people working in occupations in which board, lodging and clothing were provided saved most of their meagre earnings. A bachelor or spinster rising to the more senior levels of domestic service, such as a butler or housekeeper, could accumulate a sufficiently large sum of money over a lifetime of frugal living to justify making a will to ensure that their estate was distributed according to their wishes.

Although almost everyone remained in the social class into which they had been born, changes in relative prosperity were not uncommon. Some middle-class men, particularly merchants, became very wealthy through trade. When people from middle-class backgrounds fell on hard times, they are more likely to have had a cushion of savings to fall back on, as well as relatives able to help them out. Lower-class families could fall on hard times and into destitution fairly rapidly as a result of sudden unemployment or the untimely death or prolonged illness of a breadwinner, as well as changes brought about by factors over which they had no control such as the enclosure of land and the industrial revolution. A decline in prosperity from one generation to the next is of more significance from a genealogical perspective because a wider range of sources is likely to be available for the earlier generations who were more prosperous. From the mid-eighteenth century there was a gradual increase in economic and social divisions between yeoman farmers and agricultural labourers, at a time when the size of the population was also increasing. This could lead to a gradual decline in prosperity of younger sons of younger sons, and examples can be found of agricultural labourers in Victorian times with ancestors in the eighteenth century who were yeomen whose forebears had farmed the land they owned for generations.

Prosperity could also be affected by the inheritance of land as a result of marriage. A man of modest means might inherit land as a result of marrying the daughter of a yeoman farmer with no surviving sons. A yeoman farmer might marry a younger daughter of a family of minor gentry, who themselves might have had ancestors higher up the social scale. Yeomen and merchants might send one or more sons to Oxford or Cambridge, many of whom subsequently became Anglican clergymen. It was not uncommon for clergymen from relatively modest backgrounds to marry women from local families of minor gentry. The children of such parents would have paternal ancestors who were yeomen or merchants, but their maternal ancestors might include families listed in the visitations of the Heralds of the College of Arms in the sixteenth and seventeenth centuries.

The surviving records of many people from lower-class backgrounds, who were neither rich enough to own land nor very poor, are often minimal: in many cases limited to baptism, marriage and burial records in church registers. The main exceptions are those engaged in certain occupations and people who appeared before the courts as a result of criminal activity. People of all classes were involved in court cases, but those who appeared in the criminal courts were usually from lower-class backgrounds and often very poor. Assize and Quarter Sessions records survive in significant quantities, but although it is often possible to find information on crimes and subsequent sentences, records rarely include genealogical information, although place of birth was recorded in some prison registers. People from middle-class backgrounds, often related to each other, engaged in civil disputes over land and property in the equity courts more frequently than might be supposed, and Chancery proceedings can sometimes be a rich source of genealogical information.

Headstones are likely to have been erected after the deaths of people who were relatively prosperous, but many from the pre-Victorian period no longer survive or the inscriptions are now illegible. Memorial stones and tablets for prominent parish inhabitants and substantial landowners may have been erected inside parish churches, so have not been exposed to the elements. Wall tablets are likely still to be legible after several centuries, but floor stones may have been worn away or covered over. Some inscriptions, both inside churches and in churchyards, were recorded in the nineteenth century or earlier, quite extensively in some areas, such as Bigland's collection of Gloucestershire inscriptions, recorded in the late eighteenth century.

Sacred to the Memory of
Mrs. MARGARET MAKEPEACE,
Wife of Mr. Robert Makepeace, of London,
Citizen and Goldsmith ;
Who died the 29th of Sep., 1790, aged 61 years.
Also of the said
ROBERT MAKEPEACE, her husband,
Who died the 30th of Dec., 1800.   Aged 72 years.
Also of THOMAS, their second Son,
Who died the 12th of Sep^{r}., 1794, aged 30 years.
In the same vault lies interred all that is mortal of
ELIZABETH, the wife of Mr. Robert Makepeace,
Eldest Son of the said
Robert and Margaret Makepeace,
Who died the 30th of October, 1802, aged 32 Years.
This small tablet was erected by
Robert Makepeace, Junr., out of Gratitude and
Respect to the best of Parents and the best of Wives.
Also of ROBERT MAKEPEACE,
Son of the above-named
Robert and Margaret Makepeace,
Who having well performed the duties of this life,
Was called to his reward
On the 16th of Dec., 1827, aged 66.
This tablet was removed from the Old Chapel, 1833.

A monumental inscription recorded at Highgate church in London in 1872.

SOCIAL STATUS IN RECORDS

In the Middle Ages untitled men from the landed gentry were referred to as Esquires or gentlemen, with the former being of higher rank. Unless he was already titled, a lord of the manor was accorded the title of Esquire and was known locally as the squire. The title Esquire was also accorded to men by virtue of their occupation or office, such as barristers and Justices of the Peace. In written records Esquire was written after the name and generally abbreviated, so names appeared in the form 'John Smith, Esq.' Usage gradually changed after the late eighteenth century, so that by the twentieth century Esquire had become a form of address in written correspondence sent to men in general, although it is now rarely used.

'Gentleman' developed a dual meaning relating to social rank and standards of behaviour, but is now used almost exclusively in the latter sense. Before the nineteenth century the social status of a man as a gentleman was associated with the ownership of land and usually the absence of any association with trade. A prosperous eighteenth-century merchant could acquire a reputation for conducting himself as a gentleman in business without being considered to have the social status of a gentleman. His transformation into a gentleman by status, which may not have been achievable within his own lifetime but might be acquired by his heirs once the 'taint of trade' had been left behind, usually required buying a country estate. However, the criteria by which men were considered to be gentlemen varied considerably from one area of the country to another and from one parish to another. A yeoman was a landowner below the rank of gentleman, but in some areas yeoman farmers were referred as gentlemen where elsewhere they would have been referred to as yeomen.

The expansion of the middle class from the late eighteenth century onwards resulted in men being defined more by occupation than social origins, and 'gentleman' evolved into a classification of occupational status describing men who did not need to work, including those from modest backgrounds who had saved sufficient money during their working lives to live off in retirement. Although the meaning was never fixed at any particular time and has gradually evolved, the description of a man as a 'gent.' in records is an indication that he was not a member of the lower class.

The abbreviation 'Mr' was originally short for 'Master', with a gradual change in pronunciation. Mr denoted a man below the rank

An eighteenth-century manor house. The man who owned this house is likely to be found in records with the title 'Esquire'.

of Esquire who had authority over others, as the master of servants, employees, apprentices or pupils. A man who was a gentleman by status would be addressed as Mr, but not all men addressed as Mr had the status of gentlemen. From the late eighteenth century onwards Mr gradually evolved into a form of address for all adult males irrespective of social class. Master gradually became a form of address for boys and young men, but is rarely found in records.

Although the titles Esquire, gentleman and Mr were never precisely defined or used consistently in records at any particular time, in the pre-Victorian period they provide an important indication of social status. This can be observed in lists of parish inhabitants, such as lists of ratepayers. In a rural parish the title 'Esq.' denoted a member of the untitled landed gentry who was often a Justice of the Peace and sometimes lord of the manor, and 'Mr' denoted gentleman farmers, yeomen or tenant farmers, who employed labourers and occupied the positions of parish officers by rotation. Men listed without any title were usually tradesmen, such as blacksmiths, masons, shoemakers, wheelwrights, butchers and bakers, or agricultural labourers. Although not always recorded consistently, the presence or absence of such titles in parish registers and other records can enable individuals and families with the same surname but of different social status to be distinguished, which can be valuable in family reconstitution. People sometimes assume that everyone with the same surname living in the same parish must have been related, but it was not uncommon for families of gentry, yeomen and labourers with the same surname to have coexisted in the same parish for many generations, without any apparent connection between them.

The role of many women in the pre-Victorian period is not apparent, because in records they were usually defined in relation to their fathers or husbands. Lower-class women usually worked until they married, and may also have engaged in economic activity afterwards. Although middle-class women were rarely engaged in economic activity or business in the Victorian era, in the seventeenth and eighteenth centuries it was not uncommon for women to run their own businesses. 'Entrepreneurial widows' often continued and expanded the businesses of their late husbands, employing workers and servants, and acting as masters to apprentices.

The changes in meaning over time of the descriptions 'Mrs' and 'Miss' are explained in Erickson (2012). Mrs was originally short for 'Mistress', and was the female equivalent of Mr, signifying a woman who had authority over others, such as servants, employees, apprentices or pupils. It is important to be aware that before the mid-eighteenth century the title Mrs was not an indication of marital status but of social status. The description of a woman as 'Mrs Mary Williams' in a marriage register of this period is not an indication that she was a widow, although she may have been one, but that she was a woman of higher social status. Similarly, the title Mrs in a burial register of the same period does not imply that a woman was or had been married. From the mid-eighteenth century onwards the meaning of Mrs gradually evolved to refer to married women, but continued to be used as a title for unmarried women of higher social status in certain circumstances until the early twentieth century. Miss is another abbreviation of Mistress, which has always referred to unmarried women, but before the mid-eighteenth century was only used for young girls from families of higher social status, changing to Mrs when the girl reached adulthood or after the death of her mother, whichever came first. The title Miss was used in newspaper announcements from the mid-eighteenth century onwards to refer to young unmarried women, but is rarely found in other genealogical sources.

Chapter 6

RELIGION AND OCCUPATION

Social status, religious affiliation and occupation are three significant characteristics that define individuals, and the first two define whole families. As discussed in the previous chapter, social status usually remained constant over many generations, and this was frequently also the case with religious affiliation. Establishing that family members belonged to a particular denomination may enable them to be distinguished from others with the same surname, and the records of non-Anglican denominations can be important sources of information. Surviving educational and occupational records may also include genealogical information, as they often recorded birthplace or parentage. Occupations that ran in families for several generations can sometimes assist in distinguishing members of families with the same surname.

Although the records of non-Anglican religious denominations and occupational records sometimes include information to enable genealogical problems to be solved, their survival is very variable. Once it has been established that a person of interest was a member of a certain denomination or had a particular occupation, it is important to find out as much as possible about both the denomination or occupation itself and the extent and location of surviving records. Many books have been published on researching ancestors from specific backgrounds, including the 'My Ancestor' series published by the SoG.

RELIGIOUS AFFILIATION
The history and development of English Nonconformity is complex, and is examined from a genealogical perspective in Steel (1973). The

first wave of Nonconformity developed in the seventeenth century out of Puritanism, and consisted of the 'three denominations' of Presbyterians, Independents (Congregationalists) and Baptists, together with the Quakers (Society of Friends). The Toleration Act of 1689 allowed freedom of worship, but only applied to Protestant Dissenters, and freedom of worship was only extended to Roman Catholics over a century later in 1791. The number of Catholics in England in the seventeenth and eighteenth centuries was very small, mainly concentrated in areas with Catholic gentry, but increased significantly in the nineteenth century. Methodism developed in the eighteenth century as a movement within the Church of England and later became a separate denomination. There was a considerable growth of Nonconformity in the early nineteenth century, particularly of Methodism. It has been estimated that from the late sixteenth to the late eighteenth century well over 90 per cent of the population were nominally members of the Church of England.

Nonconformity tended to be concentrated in specific areas, particularly in towns and cities, but also in certain rural areas. In the eighteenth century many members of Independent, Presbyterian and Quaker congregations were from middle-class backgrounds, including merchants and craftsmen, but Baptists were more likely to be from lower-class backgrounds. People tended not only to remain members of the religious denomination into which they had been born but also to marry others of the same denomination. This was a strict requirement for Quakers, and those marrying non-Quakers, referred to as 'marrying out', were usually disowned and expelled. The expectation or requirement to marry someone of the same denomination sometimes resulted in marriages between people living some distance apart. In 1739 George Goundry of Bishop Auckland in Co. Durham married Phoebe Watson of Allendale in Northumberland, some 35 miles away, at the Quaker meeting house in Allendale, after which they lived in the Bishop Auckland area.

With the exception of Quakers, Nonconformists were required by law to marry in the Church of England between 1754 and 1837, and Probert (2012) has confirmed that this was also the norm before

1754, when to be legally valid a marriage had to be performed by an Anglican clergyman. Quakers held their own marriage ceremonies from the seventeenth century onwards, although there were doubts about their legal validity that persisted until the nineteenth century. The first appearance of someone born into a Quaker family in Church of England records is often a marriage record in which they married a non-Quaker. John Goundry, the son of George Goundry and Phoebe Watson mentioned above, married Mary Castle at the parish church of Heighington in Co. Durham in 1781. John was subsequently disowned by the Quakers, as recorded in the minutes of Bishop Auckland Monthly Meeting. All four of John Goundry's grandparents had been born into Quaker families and can be traced in Quaker records.

A Quaker meeting for worship. Quakers were renowned for keeping detailed and accurate records.

The children of Independent and Presbyterian parents are likely to have been baptized, but not all churches kept records and some records were kept by individual ministers, and were subsequently lost. The survival of early baptism records of Presbyterian and Independent congregations is very variable, as is the survival of records of births and adult baptisms in Baptist congregations, which did not practise infant baptism. The Quakers, in contrast, kept meticulous records, including recording the births, deaths and marriages of members, and the survival of these records is good. As a result of a tax on the registering of births, deaths and marriages, the births of Nonconformists were recorded in parish registers in the period from 1695 to 1706, and this practice was continued in some parishes in later periods. These records may enable a family to be identified as Nonconformists, particularly when no records of the relevant congregation have survived for the period.

Some Nonconformist congregations met in private houses or meeting houses and not all churches had burial grounds, so many Nonconformists were buried in the local parish churchyard. The presence of marriages and burials for a surname in the parish register but the absence of any corresponding baptisms is a strong indication that the family was Nonconformist. The absence of records for some Nonconformist congregations in the early and mid-eighteenth century can be illustrated with reference to Westbury in Wiltshire. Baptist and Independent congregations were established there in 1662. The Independents are estimated to have comprised half of Westbury's population in the early eighteenth century, including some of the town's most influential inhabitants. Many children would not have been baptized in the parish church, but there are no surviving baptism records for the Baptists until 1762 or for the Independents until 1769.

Some Nonconformist churches had procedures for the transfer of members from one congregation to another. This sometimes involved issuing the departing member with a certificate to be presented to the new congregation. The issuing and receipt of such certificates was sometimes recorded in church minute books, so it

Westbury parish church, Wiltshire. In the early eighteenth century many prominent Westbury inhabitants were Nonconformists, so their children were not baptized here.

Westbury Independent Chapel (now United Reformed Church), Wiltshire. This chapel was rebuilt in 1821, but an Independent congregation had existed in Westbury since 1662. No registers of baptisms survive before 1769.

may be possible to establish the relocation of an individual or family from one area to another. Quakers had an elaborate system for providing references for members moving to another area. Monthly Meetings issued certificates to members to take with them to the new Monthly Meeting, and the issuing and receipt of certificates was recorded in Monthly Meeting minutes.

Most surviving Nonconformist birth, baptism, death and burial registers before 1837 were deposited with the Registrar General in the nineteenth century and are now held at TNA, and these have been digitized and indexed online. Some registers were not deposited with the Registrar General, and remained in the custody of churches. Most of these, together with other surviving records of Nonconformist congregations, including those of an administrative nature, which may record the names of members, have now been deposited in local archives.

Published county and local histories can provide information on the prevalence of Nonconformity in particular areas and the locations of major congregations. Some local archives and family history societies have produced lists of Nonconformist congregations and their surviving records. The *National Index of Parish Registers*, a series of volumes covering some counties and published by the SoG several years ago, may also be useful in identifying Nonconformist records.

The Presbyterian Church of England and the Congregational Church in England and Wales amalgamated to form the United Reformed Church (URC) in 1972. Records in local archives relating to former Independent and Presbyterian congregations that are now part of the United Reformed Church may therefore be listed under the names of present-day URC churches.

OCCUPATION

Occupation was not routinely recorded in baptism registers before 1813, in marriage registers before 1837, or in burial registers at all, but was recorded in all three types of register in some parishes during various earlier periods.

Some occupations tended to run in families, particularly skilled trades such as blacksmiths and tailors. Such trades were learned through apprenticeship, but formal apprenticeship agreements were not always drawn up. Families involved in established trades often remained in the same town or village for many generations. Churchwardens and overseers of the poor employed a range of local tradesmen, and surviving records may include their names and occupations. The occupations likely to be recorded include carpenters, masons, blacksmiths, tailors, shoemakers, carriers (carters), butchers and bakers. As well as being rich sources of family history information, such records can often provide clues to genealogical relationships and corroborate information found in parish registers.

Detailed records for certain professions and occupations were maintained, particularly of people employed in the service of the church and state. The survival rate of such records is generally good and they are often quite extensive from the late eighteenth century onwards and sometimes earlier. With the exception of soldiers and sailors, most occupations for which records were kept and have survived are those engaged in by men from middle-class backgrounds. These include Anglican clergymen, who were almost all graduates of Oxford and Cambridge, lawyers, physicians, Customs and Excise officers, and craftsmen and merchants who became freemen of the City of London and of some other towns and cities. Some occupational sources record the place and date or year of birth and others record the various places in which an employee served, enabling the birthplaces of children to be established.

Many provincial towns had craft and other guilds. Members of guilds in towns, and of trade and craft associations in London known as livery companies, could become freemen, usually in one of three ways: by patrimony (if their father was a freeman), by servitude (serving as an apprentice to a freeman), or by redemption (purchase). In London freedom of the City of London could only be obtained by a man who had obtained the freedom of a livery company. Apprenticeship records and lists of freemen for many town and cities have survived. These records often include genealogical information, including the name and abode of the father, and some lists of freemen and apprentices have been published.

Identifying occupations before 1813 can be difficult, and it is therefore advisable to examine as many records as possible that relate, or could relate, to the family concerned. A possible baptism record was found for Mary Bludwick at Great Hormead, Hertfordshire, in 1728, daughter of Richard and Mary Bludwick. Baptism records for three possible siblings were also found, including one for Elizabeth Bludwick at Royston a year later, which recorded the occupation of Richard Bludwick as an 'exciseman'. This was an important clue enabling Richard Bludwick's career to be traced in the Excise Board minute books held at TNA. These not only provided evidence that the baptism found for Mary Bludwick must be the correct one but also enabled further clues to Richard Bludwick's ancestry to be found. Although occupation was not recorded in the majority of pre-1813 records, it was recorded occasionally. Attempting to rely on index-only records in this period on the assumption that little further information was recorded in original records can therefore result in vital clues being missed.

The occupations of men born in the late eighteenth century but who had no children baptized after 1813 can sometimes be obtained from death records after 1837. Although death records for adult males contain little or no genealogical information, they do include occupation. This can sometimes enable occupational records to be identified, which may enable the origins of some men who died after 1837 but before 1851 to be established. Occupations recorded in death records were not always the same as those recorded in censuses, so a man might be recorded in the 1841 census as a labourer, but in a death record as a Chelsea Pensioner, a clue that is likely to enable his place of birth to be established from army records. Death records for married women and widows recorded the names and occupations of their husbands. The death record of a widow who died after 1837, and may have outlived her husband by many years, can provide information on the occupation of a man who had died some time before 1837.

The meanings of some words indicating the occupations or other characteristics of adult males have changed over time, as in the following examples:

• A 'clerk' was rarely someone who worked in an office keeping records and filing papers, but was usually a clergyman or 'clerk in holy orders'.

• A man referred to as a 'pensioner' was not receiving a state old-age pension, as these were not introduced until the early twentieth century, but was usually a former soldier or sailor receiving a pension for disability or long service from Chelsea or Greenwich Hospitals, although not necessarily living there. Before the twentieth century a person living on what would today be regarded as a private pension, usually derived from income from investments, land or property, would be referred to as an 'annuitant' or 'living on own means' or 'independent means' or sometimes as a 'gentleman'. A poor elderly person receiving regular parish relief under the Poor Law would be referred to as a 'pauper'. The term 'superannuated' was used for some former government employees in receipt of occupational pensions, such as Customs and Excise officers. A pensioner at the University of Cambridge, however, was a student who paid for his board and lodging.

• The term 'commoner' referred to anyone who was not a member of the nobility, but was used by Burke to refer to the untitled landed gentry when he published *A History of the Commoners*, subsequently changed to *A History of the Landed Gentry*. A commoner was also a student at the University of Oxford not receiving an exhibition or scholarship.

• An 'invalid' was not usually a man suffering from a long-term debilitating illness, but a soldier no longer fit for active army service although capable of garrison duties during times of war.

APPRENTICESHIP
Apprenticeships involved the parents of a child, usually a boy, paying a sum of money, known as a premium, to a master to enable the

child to learn a trade or craft for a fixed number of years. This was only possible if families could afford to pay, and future prospects could be improved through apprenticeships in higher-status occupations. This sometimes involved taking up an apprenticeship in a local town or city, and boys from all parts of the country were apprenticed to a wide range of trades, crafts and professions in London. Apprenticeships were undertaken to enter not only skilled trades and crafts, but also those that are now regarded as professions, such as surgeons, apothecaries and attorneys. Boys were usually apprenticed at the age of 14, for a term of seven years, with the apprenticeship lasting until at least the age of 21. In London apprenticeships were controlled by livery companies. There was not necessarily a connection between the trade or craft in which a boy was apprenticed and the livery company of which he later became a member. This divergence became more common as time went on, so a man may not always be found in the records of the expected livery company. Although the majority of apprentices in provincial towns were from the surrounding area, between half and three-quarters of London apprentices were from outside the capital and many were from some distance away. London apprenticeship records can therefore be an important source for establishing a person's origins in another part of the country. Further information on apprenticeship records can be found in Raymond (2010). Parish apprenticeships, under the Poor Law, were quite different, as they were usually in lowly occupations that did not lead to any improvement in economic circumstances and were arranged for girls as well as boys.

EDUCATION
Before the state became involved in the provision of education in 1870, some lower-class children received an elementary education in parish or charity schools, but only a very small proportion of the population, mainly boys, were educated at secondary level or above. Many upper-class boys had private tutors. Upper- and middle-class girls rarely attended school but learned 'accomplishments' at home.

Schools providing secondary-level education consisted of what are now known as public schools, mostly boarding institutions, which educated the sons of the gentry and aristocracy, and local endowed grammar schools, which served their local area and educated mainly middle-class boys. Many young men born into middle- and upper-class families attended university. Oxford and Cambridge were the only universities in England until the early nineteenth century, and many graduates were subsequently ordained as Anglican clergymen. Some young men attended one of the four universities in Scotland, Trinity College Dublin and universities in Europe. Other young men trained as lawyers at the Inns of Court in London. Records of university alumni and the Inns of Court have generally survived, and in many cases record father's name, abode and age at entry. Various lists have been published and many are now searchable online. Records often survive for what are now public schools and some lists of former pupils have been published.

Chapter 7

RELOCATION

The availability of census data generally enables the relocation of individuals and families living in the Victorian period to be established relatively easily, whether involving migration to a nearby parish 3 miles away, to a town or city 30 miles away, or to a completely different area 300 miles away. The 1851 census recorded the exact birthplace of each individual, but information on birthplace had rarely been recorded previously. When researching ancestral lines back in time some people seem to suddenly appear out of nowhere, but this is not necessarily an indication of relocation, as it can also be the result of defective records in the areas where they had been born, which is discussed further in Chapter 12. Despite the absence of census records in the pre-Victorian period, it is sometimes possible to identify a person's place of origin using other sources. There are many reasons why people moved to other locations in Great Britain in the past, referred to by historians and historical demographers as *internal migration*. Some of the reasons for relocation in the pre-Victorian period are discussed in this chapter, together with sources and techniques that may enable evidence of relocation to be found.

REASONS FOR RELOCATION
Whyte (2000) provides a summary of research on the topic of internal migration from the perspective of a historical geographer. Although internal migration during earlier periods is now believed to have been more common than was once thought, the rate increased from the mid-eighteenth century. Agrarian reforms and the enclosure of

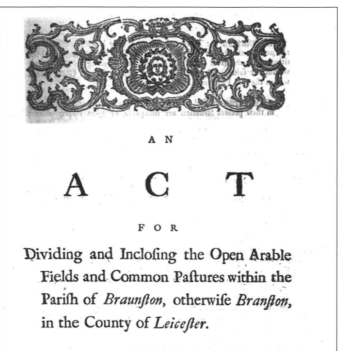

An enclosure act from 1766. The enclosure of land accelerated after the mid-eighteenth century.

land resulted in many poor agricultural labourers leaving their home parishes to seek work elsewhere, and the industrial revolution drew people to new types of work, often in areas where water power or coal were readily available.

Before the Victorian age and the development of railways, people employed in most lower-class occupations usually travelled on foot, and it was not unusual for labourers to walk several miles to work. Although people from middle-class backgrounds could afford to use horses or horse-drawn transport, travel on land was constrained not only by the speed of horses but also by the condition of the roads, so journeys between coastal towns were frequently made by sea. The condition of the roads between towns was generally poor until the building of new turnpike toll roads in the late eighteenth century, resulting in the reduction of journey times and an increase in travel by stagecoach. Although some people from lower-class backgrounds rarely if ever left their home parishes, travel was a regular feature of the lives of others, including the servants of some upper-class families, soldiers, sailors, and men employed in the transport of goods, people and animals.

Relocation sometimes took place to new areas where the economic prospects were better, referred to as *betterment migration*. The first stage in betterment migration for some young men involved leaving their home area to take up an apprenticeship in a higher-status occupation or to attend university. Most relocation by lower-class families was for economic reasons, often resulting from factors over which they had little or no control, and with no significant advantage in income or status, referred to as *subsistence migration*. People may have been forced to move because the prospects for work were poor or non-existent in the area in which they were living, particularly in the period from 1750 to 1850 when the population more than doubled. For an agricultural labourer, whether single or married, this might mean moving to another area where agricultural work was more plentiful, or to an industrial or mining area where different types of labouring work were available. If the amount of work available in the new area subsequently decreased, or the wages were low, the individual or family might move again. Young unmarried people, particularly women, often moved from agricultural areas to towns and cities to work as domestic servants, but sometimes returned to their home parishes

Sheffield in 1819. Migration to towns accelerated as a result of the industrial revolution.

following marriage. Subsistence migration often involved relocation within a radius of about 30 miles, but sometimes much longer distances were involved.

Social historians have developed the concept of open and closed rural parishes. In *closed parishes* a significant proportion of the land was owned by one or two landlords. In some closed parishes there was one resident landlord or squire living in the 'big house', who was often the lord of the manor and a magistrate. Other closed parishes had an absentee landlord, with the land leased to one or more tenant farmers. In both cases the population was usually low and remained relatively stable. The main economic activity was usually agriculture and there was little or no industry. There was little Nonconformity, and often an expectation that parishioners would attend church, so children were usually baptized in infancy. There was a high level of economic and social stratification, but the poorer inhabitants, whose ancestors may have lived in the parish for several generations, were often treated relatively humanely if they fell on hard times. There was little migration into such parishes, but it was sometimes necessary for young people born into large families to leave to seek work elsewhere.

In *open parishes* there were many smaller landowners, with small- and medium-sized farms, no big house and no squire, and there were often crafts and industries as well as farms. Families were able to move into such parishes when work was available, but could be removed to their parish of settlement under the Poor Law if they fell on hard times. Relatively few new Anglican churches were built before the 1820s to cope with the increasing population, so low levels of church attendance were common and Nonconformity often flourished. The children of lower-class parents, who were not necessarily regular church-goers, were not always baptized in infancy. Open parishes in rural areas resembled parishes in towns and cities rather than closed rural parishes.

Under the Poor Law, people were sometimes sent back to places they had previously lived, or to places where they had never lived at all if they had inherited a parish of settlement from a husband or father. Criteria for obtaining a settlement in a parish included paying rent of £10 or more per annum, serving an apprenticeship, or being hired to work for a year and a day. Some long-term residents, such as agricultural day labourers, could have lived and worked in a parish for many years but not obtained a settlement there because they had not fulfilled any of the relevant criteria. A woman took the settlement of her husband on marriage, and children took the settlement of their father until such time as they obtained a settlement of their own. If a man or an unmarried woman had not fulfilled any criteria to obtain their own settlement, they inherited the settlement of their father. A widow retained her late husband's settlement, but might not be certain of the details of what it was or how her husband had obtained it. She could therefore potentially have a settlement based on that of her father-in-law, or even her late husband's grandfather.

When people applied for poor relief, referred to as becoming 'chargeable', their parish of settlement was responsible for providing for them. In most cases, if they were not living in their parish of settlement they would be removed there, but in some cases the parish of settlement agreed to pay the costs involved in their maintenance, particularly for short periods. Disputes between parishes over settlement were common, and were referred to Quarter Sessions for a final decision. Understanding the operation of the Old Poor Law in the period before 1834 and the records that were generated is very important when carrying out research on lower-class families in the pre-Victorian period. Most books describing genealogical sources provide some background information on the Old Poor Law, and Tate (2011) and Hawkings (2011) both cover the topic in some detail.

Relocation at regular intervals was a characteristic of certain occupations, as it is today. During peacetime, soldiers, both officers and other ranks, were subject to postings of varying duration at home and overseas. Other employees of the state, such as Customs and Excise officers, were also subject to frequent change of location. Servants employed by upper-class families who owned multiple landed estates could work in different places at different times. Wealthy families employed both indoor servants such as maids and cooks and outdoor servants such as gardeners, grooms, coachmen and gamekeepers. Personal servants such as valets and lady's maids usually accompanied their employers on their travels. Temporary relocation in the service of an employer could improve the chances of finding alternative employment, a marriage partner, or both, and result in people leaving their old employment and settling in new areas.

The century after 1815 is characterized by a long period of relative peace that came to an end in 1914, but during the period from 1756 to 1815 the country was at war for more years than it was at peace. The major wars were:

Seven Years War (1756–1763)
American War of Independence (1775–1783) and war with France (1778–1783)
French Revolutionary War (1793–1802)
Napoleonic War (1803–1815) and war with the United States (1812–1815).

During periods of war the size of the army and navy mushroomed, with men serving both in the British Isles and overseas. The militia was a force of part-time soldiers that was called up for full-time service when the country was at war. Men were selected to serve in the militia by ballot, but had the option to provide a substitute or pay for one to be provided. The 'New Militia' was established in 1757, and during periods of war the English county militia regiments served in strategic locations throughout Great Britain, usually outside their county of origin. They were not obliged to serve in Ireland, but several regiments volunteered to do so during the Irish Rebellion of 1798. Employment in the Royal Dockyards, at Plymouth, Portsmouth, Sheerness, Chatham, Woolwich and Deptford, also increased during times of war, drawing in workers from the surrounding areas and further afield.

Great Britain was almost continuously at war during the twenty-two years from 1793 to 1815, when a higher proportion of the male population served in the armed forces than at any time until the First World War, with many men serving away from home. There was a brief interval of peace between the French Revolutionary War and the Napoleonic War following the Peace of Amiens in March 1802, when large numbers of men were discharged from the army and navy and the militia was stood down, so many men returned home and many people from the middle and upper classes took the opportunity to travel to Europe and visit Paris. The resumption of hostilities in May 1803 resulted in renewed mass enlistment into the army and navy and re-embodiment of the militia. The wives and families of soldiers and militiamen often accompanied their husbands, and children were sometimes born in areas where their fathers were serving. Unmarried soldiers and militiamen sometimes met their future wives while serving away from home, and couples often settled in the home area of either the wife or husband. Large numbers of men were discharged from the army and navy after 1815, swelling the ranks of the unemployed, and resulting in migration to areas where work was more plentiful.

British soldiers during the Napoleonic era. Great Britain was almost continuously at war from 1793 to 1815.

EVIDENCE OF RELOCATION

Local listings made in connection with the decennial censuses from 1801 to 1831 occasionally survive, as well as earlier listings of inhabitants compiled for a variety of purposes from the sixteenth century onwards, described in general books on genealogical sources. Some recorded only the name of the head of household together with the number of people, but others listed all members of a household, and some indicated relationships and ages. Other lists of parish inhabitants, such as Hearth Tax returns and militia ballot lists, were produced for specific purposes and listed individuals who fulfilled certain criteria. Such listings, referred to by genealogical researchers as *census substitutes*, can be of great value when they exist, but unlike later censuses they rarely recorded place of birth.

Establishing the relocation of a whole family within a relatively small geographical area based entirely on baptism, marriage and burial records is more likely to be possible in areas where the population density was low and the surname was uncommon, distinctive Christian names or naming patterns were used, and children were baptized either in the Church of England or in a Nonconformist denomination whose records have survived for the relevant period. The spacing between the baptisms of children with the same parents' names in different parishes can often provide a clue as to whether one or more couples were involved. Two baptisms within a few months of each other in different parishes are likely to relate to two different couples, but there is a slight possibility that they could relate to only one couple if one or both was a late baptism.

John Castle of Ayton married Elizabeth Thomson of Eston on 22 January 1715 at Ingleby Greenhow in the North Riding of Yorkshire, after which children were baptized in five different parishes within a 10-mile radius during the following two decades:

Ann Castle	22 May 1716	Great Ayton
John Castle	10 December 1717	Marton
Mary Castle	8 December 1719	Ormesby
William Castle	22 January 1722	Guisborough

Francis Castle	4 February 1724	Great Ayton
Elizabeth Castle	14 April 1726	Stainton
James Castle	2 May 1728	Stainton
Robert Castle	31 January 1732	Great Ayton
Richard Castle	10 June 1734	Stokesley

Although some of these parishes are now on the fringe of industrial Teesside, in the early eighteenth century the area was very sparsely populated, so there can be little doubt that all these baptisms relate to children of the same couple.

It may also be possible to obtain evidence for the relocation of a whole family over a much longer distance using the technique of family reconstitution, by correlating the baptism, marriage and burial records in the parish of origin with those in the destination parish for the whole family to a sufficiently high level of confidence that no other explanation could be possible. This is more likely to be feasible if the family had an uncommon surname, one or more family members had uncommon Christian names, and the number of children in the generation that migrated was relatively large. In the latter case the larger number of family members for whom events can be correlated reduces the possibility of confusion with other families having the same surname. Naming patterns may also provide corroborating evidence, for example if Christian names of children in the destination parish reflected those of grandparents and other family members in the parish of origin.

Establishing the relocation of only one person, unless they had a very distinctive combination of Christian name and surname, usually requires corroborating evidence from sources other than church registers. Further evidence can sometimes be found in education, apprenticeship, employment and Poor Law records. For people who could sign their names, distinctive signatures in records in the area of origin and the destination area may provide evidence of relocation. Signatures as a source of evidence are discussed in Chapter 10.

Information on the birthplace or earlier place of abode of parents was recorded in baptism registers in some parts of the country in the late eighteenth and early nineteenth centuries, particularly in the north of England. Most of these registers came to an end in 1813 when the new printed registers were introduced, but some parishes continued the old system in parallel with the new for several years, or continued to record more information in the printed registers than was required. Many parishes in the Diocese of York kept more detailed registers from 1777 known as 'Dade' registers after William Dade, the York curate who devised the system. Registers in parishes that adopted the system are extremely detailed, often recording the names and abodes of grandparents, but many parishes refused to adopt the system and the Archbishop of York was unwilling to enforce it. In the Diocese of Durham, including most of Durham and Northumberland, detailed registers were kept in almost all parishes for the period from 1798 to 1812 and are known as 'Barrington' registers, after the Bishop of Durham, Shute Barrington.

Hannah Gibbons was baptized at Sunderland in Co. Durham in 1785, the daughter of William and Elizabeth Gibbons. William Gibbons married Elizabeth Keen at Sunderland in 1784 and nine children were baptized there between 1785 and 1809. The more detailed 'Barrington' baptism records after 1798 confirm the mother's maiden surname as Keen and record the place of origin of both parents. The baptism record of the last child on 10 September 1809 contains the following information:

> Peter Gibbons, born 11 July 1809, 6th son of William Gibbons, labourer, native of Moreland by his wife Elizabeth Keen, native of Appleby.

Elizabeth Keen had been baptized at Appleby in Westmorland in 1766, the daughter of Arthur Keen, the sergeant in the Westmorland Militia whose ancestry was discussed in Chapter 2. The information in the baptism records for the younger siblings of Hannah Gibbons therefore enabled the places of birth of her parents to be established and their baptisms to be traced. As can be seen from this example, a more detailed baptism record may enable a genealogical problem relating to a sibling to be solved, even though the person who is the focus of research was born before or after the period during which the more detailed records were made.

Children born during the period from 1793 to 1815 may have been born and baptized away from their home area if their father was serving in the army or militia. For people still alive in 1851, clues to births in locations relating to military service may be found in the 1851 census. The locations in which soldiers and militiamen served can be established using service records for men who were awarded pensions, which are available online, and in muster rolls held at TNA, so it may be possible to find evidence from military records that children with the same parents' names but baptized in different areas must have been siblings. Following a soldier's career is usually much easier if he was awarded a pension, and is otherwise dependent on establishing the name of the regiment so that the relevant muster rolls can be identified and searched. The father's occupation was routinely recorded in baptism registers from 1813, and for soldiers usually included the name of the regiment. On 6 February 1813, for example, the following baptism was recorded at St Andrew, Plymouth:

> Charles, son of John and Elizabeth Meyrick, Plymouth, Musician, Shropshire Militia

Strong links between regular army regiments and specific counties only developed in the 1870s, so the name of the regiment in which a man served rarely provides any clues to the county where he had been recruited. However, militiamen usually served in the regiment of the county in which they normally resided, which in the majority of cases was their county of birth. Although muster rolls of the embodied militia are held at TNA, other records of county militias are held in local archives, which often list individual militiamen, and may include details of their parish of origin or birth.

Lists of the names of parish inhabitants paying taxes and rates, such as land tax assessments, lists of ratepayers, overseers' accounts and churchwardens' accounts, contain little or no genealogical information, but changes in the names recorded over a period of time may provide clues to arrivals in the parish or departures from it.

Poor Law records often provide evidence or clues relating to previous abode. Settlement examinations are extremely valuable in establishing the origins of poor people who moved from parish to parish, particularly if they were recorded for two successive generations of a family at the same time. Abraham Everett senior and Abraham Everett junior had both become chargeable to the parish of Kingsbury Episcopi in Somerset in 1831, and were examined at Ilminster Petty Sessions to establish their parish of settlement. As well as further details of the course of their lives, both records include information about their origins. Abraham Everett senior stated:

> I am about 70 year of age and was born as I believe at Corscomb in the County of Dorset.

Abraham Everett junior stated:

> I was born as I believe at Coker [Somerset] and am about 34 years of age. I was married about 14 years ago at Whimple in the County of Devon to Susan my present wife by whom I have six children, Sarah about eleven years old, John about nine years old, Isaac about seven years old, Elizabeth about five years old, Louisa about three years old and Alfred about two years old.

Clues to former places of abode or the location of family members may be found in wills, particularly of people from middle-class backgrounds who may have owned land. Testators sometimes expressed a desire to be buried in a specific church or grave. In her will, proved in 1760 at the Archdeaconry Court of Northampton,

Elizabeth Wilkins of Brackley stated that she wished to be buried in the parish church at Edmonton near London, either in the same grave as her husband, Robert Wilkins, or that of her son Thomas. This indicates that the family had a connection with the London area, and enabled the relevant burial records to be identified. Establishing the place of burial and the dates of the deaths of Robert and Thomas Wilkins enabled their wills to be traced more easily than would otherwise have been possible.

Monumental inscriptions sometimes recorded a place of birth or usual place of abode. Inscriptions that were recorded in the nineteenth century and earlier can be particularly valuable. An inscription for Robert Wilkins at Edmonton was recorded in a published collection of Middlesex inscriptions made by Frederick Teague Cansick in the 1870s:

Here lieth the Body of Mr Robert Wilkins late of Brackley in Northampton Shire who departed this life Feb the 6th 1712. In the 45th Year of his Age

A former place of abode was often recorded in deeds when people purchased, mortgaged or leased property. Edward Spencer was a yeoman farmer who died in 1823 at Newton St Loe in Somerset, aged 55, so he had been born about 1768. His baptism could not be found in any of the surrounding parishes in Somerset, and no relevant wills could be traced because those proved in Somerset were destroyed in the Exeter Blitz of 1942. The place of birth of Edward Spencer was established from a lease dated 1793 in a collection of deeds held at Somerset Heritage Centre relating to Newton St Loe, in which one of the parties was named as 'John Spencer & Edward Spencer sons of Thomas Spencer of Little Chalfield, Wiltshire, yeoman'. This and other deeds confirmed that Edward Spencer was the son of Thomas Spencer of Little Chalfield in Wiltshire, some 10 miles from Newton St Loe, and a record of his baptism was found there in 1768.

ABSENCE OVERSEAS

Some people who subsequently lived in England had been born overseas, and others, although they were born and died in England, spent considerable periods of their lives abroad. Emigration, mainly to British colonies, took place from the early seventeenth century onwards. In most cases this was betterment migration by people who possessed the financial resources to pay for their own passage, or agreed to work as indentured servants for a specified number of years in exchange for the payment of their passage. It is not always appreciated that there was always a reverse flow, and a proportion of emigrants eventually returned to Great Britain, in the majority of cases to the place they had left.

Emigration to North America increased rapidly in the 1760s and early 1770s until the outbreak of the American War of Independence. Historians estimate that only 40–45 per cent of American colonists supported the war, with 15–20 per cent opposed to independence and the remainder seeking to remain neutral and avoid getting involved. During and after the war many of those who did not wish to remain in the United States relocated to other British colonies, particularly Canada, and others returned to Great Britain.

Some men, including soldiers and officers of the British army, and military and civil service employees of the Honourable East India Company (HEIC), served overseas, often with their families. If an individual or family apparently disappears there is the possibility that they lived overseas for a period of time and that one or more children were born there. Service of this nature, particularly in the case of army officers, often ran in families, so more than one generation was sometimes born overseas. Clues to overseas residence can sometimes be found in wills, deeds and other records. Information on tracing baptisms, marriages and deaths that occurred overseas can be found in a guide published by the Guildhall Library (1995). The failure to find a burial because a person died overseas or at sea is discussed in Chapter 12.

Chapter 8

SEARCHING FOR INFORMATION

In post-1837 research it is often possible to harvest a significant amount of 'low-hanging fruit' using only one online subscription service providing access to only two major genealogical sources: the GRO indexes and the decennial censuses. In contrast, the solution of genealogical problems in the pre-Victorian period frequently requires information from a range of sources, not necessarily available or searchable online. Research on the ancestry of people with certain occupations or who belonged to particular religious denominations may require using very specific sources that researchers have not previously used. Online genealogical search services, whether free or requiring payment, should now be regarded simply as collections of miscellaneous derivative sources. Other relevant sources may only be available in specific archives, or sometimes as microfilm copies available in more than one location.

The first stage in seeking a solution to a genealogical problem in the pre-Victorian period is to identify all the sources in which information could potentially be found and establish how they can be accessed. Selection of relevant sources is dependent what is already known about the family concerned, and should take into account factors discussed in previous chapters, such as social status, religious affiliation and occupation. If a family clearly came from a middle-class background, searching for the wills of family members would be appropriate at an early stage. This requires an understanding of the hierarchy of probate courts in the relevant area, as explained in Raymond (2012) and Gibson and Raymond (2016). If a family is known to have been very poor, searching for relevant

Poor Law records would be appropriate. This requires not only an understanding of the operation of the Poor Law, but also an appreciation of any boundary changes that may have affected the current location of records, as explained in Chapter 9.

The process of searching for information can be represented in Figure 1.

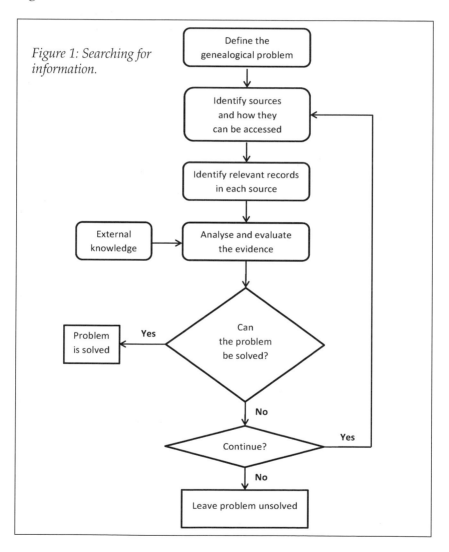

Figure 1: Searching for information.

Relevant records in sources can be identified using online search tools, various other types of search tool not available online, and by browsing systematically through the records in original sources or photographic facsimiles, as represented in Figure 2. Potential sources of genealogical information are often quite large in extent, but in the absence of available search tools it may still be possible to identify relevant records by systematic browsing, as was frequently necessary for searching many sources before indexes became available. Locating an individual or family in the censuses before they were indexed by name, for example, required using clues from other sources to identify areas in which they were likely to have lived and then browsing the schedules street by street. Similarly, when seeking information in unindexed sources, it may be possible to limit the amount of browsing required in sources arranged geographically if the approximate location can be established, and in sources arranged chronologically if the approximate date can be estimated.

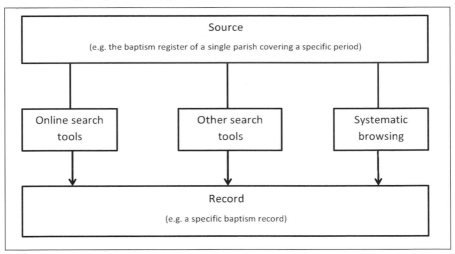

Figure 2: Identifying records in sources.

The feasibility of browsing through an unindexed source is dependent on its size and is also influenced by the probability of finding relevant records. Whether a researcher can justify the time spent browsing through a large unindexed source when there is no guarantee that anything will be found is ultimately a personal decision depending on the time they have available and their persistence in trying to solve a genealogical problem.

TYPES OF SEARCH TOOL

Search tools, sometimes referred to as finding aids, comprise a wide range of different types of catalogue and index in various formats, which enable specific records to be identified in sources. Genealogical research usually involves searching for specific names, often in specific locations. It is therefore important to identify all the search tools available for the relevant geographical area. The *GENUKI* website can be very useful in identifying the search tools available for some counties, and often those relevant to specific parishes, but this is a volunteer project so the amount of information varies considerably from one county to another. The main categories of search tool are as follows:

• Large online search services covering the whole country, but with varying coverage by county, comprising both subscription services such as Ancestry, Findmypast and The Genealogist, and free services such as FamilySearch and FreeReg.
• Commercial online search services focusing on specific geographical areas, such as Durham Records Online.
• Online databases and other resources available only to the members of family history societies, sometimes at additional cost, such as the Cornwall Family History Society's research database.
• Printed indexes, such as the British Record Society's indexes of wills, some of which are also now searchable online.
• Indexes produced by family history societies, individuals and local publishers, in the form of booklets, microfiche, CDs and downloadable files, which can be purchased directly from the publisher or from online vendors such as GENfair and Parish Chest and are sometimes also available in archives and libraries.
• Manuscript and typescript indexes, often produced several decades

ago, and available at only one or two specific locations, usually the relevant archive or local studies library and/or the SoG in London.

• Archive catalogues, discussed in the next chapter.

• Unique search tools available at specific locations, such as card indexes in archives and local studies libraries.

• 'Archival' indexes produced during the same time period as the records to which they relate, and having an original day-to-day function as search tools. Indexes of this type are usually held in archives, either available in searchrooms or stored with the relevant record collections. These indexes are often *alphabets* (arranged under the first letter of a surname rather than in strict alphabetical order) to volumes that recorded events in chronological order.

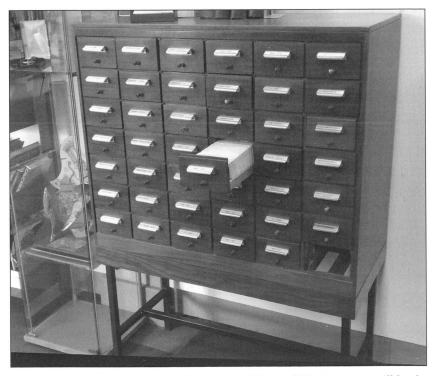

A traditional card index. Card indexes in archives and libraries may still be the only search tools available for some sources.

ONLINE SEARCH SERVICES

Large online search services such as Ancestry and Findmypast provide access to a wide range of genealogical sources, including church registers, monumental inscriptions, probate records, Poor Law records, educational and occupational records, criminal records and military records. Each online search service comprises multiple *record collections*, with the term 'record' used in the computing and information retrieval context to refer to database records. The content of each record collection is usually one of the following:

• *index-only records*: database records containing only the names of the people referred to in the corresponding original records
• *full or partial transcriptions*: database records containing the names of the people referred to, together with some or all of the additional information from original records
• *indexed images*: database records containing the names of the people referred to, linked to digital images of original sources
• *unindexed images*: browsable collections of digital images of original sources.

Many record collections relevant to the pre-Victorian period are available through only one online search service. Parish registers and other sources held in local archives have usually been digitized as a result of contracts between archive services and specific online search services. For example, Devon parish registers have been digitized by Findmypast but those for neighbouring Dorset and Somerset by Ancestry. Most parish registers for the Greater London area, held at London Metropolitan Archives, have been digitized by Ancestry, but those held at City of Westminster Archives by Findmypast. Norfolk parish registers, however, have been digitized by three different online search services: Findmypast, The Genealogist and Ancestry, and non-exclusive licences may become more common in the future. Access to more than one online subscription service is usually necessary when carrying out research in the pre-Victorian period, but it may not be necessary to take out a personal subscription to services only used occasionally, as free access may be available in public libraries, local archives, LDS family history centres and the research centres of local family history societies.

The majority of record collections produced by family history societies are only available through Findmypast, as a result of a partnership with the Federation of Family History Societies. Many of these collections were produced as search tools before large-scale digitization projects became technically feasible or economically viable, and comprise index-only records or transcriptions, without links to images.

Several major genealogical sources held at TNA have been digitized by Ancestry, Findmypast, The Genealogist and by TNA itself. In the latter case, records can be identified using the *Discovery* catalogue (see Chapter 9) and images downloaded for a small charge.

FamilySearch is a free online search service provided by the LDS, which developed out of the earlier International Genealogical Index (IGI). The searchable content comprises index-only records, mainly of baptisms and marriages, from sources microfilmed by the LDS, together with some information submitted by individuals. FamilySearch has established partnerships with certain online subscription services to share information, with the result that some records on FamilySearch include links to images on partner websites (requiring a subscription for access), and Findmypast and Ancestry include collections of baptism and marriage records supplied by the LDS that are also searchable free of charge on FamilySearch.

When searching Ancestry and Findmypast it is not uncommon for a search for an event, such as a baptism or marriage, to result in the retrieval of two or more database records corresponding to the same original historical record. These database records may be derived from:

• parish register digitization projects
• LDS indexes of baptisms and marriages
• family history societies' databases (mainly on Findmypast).

Duplicate indexing by different organizations may enable a record to be identified even when one index contains a transcription error. Whenever a record cannot be found in an expected record collection, it is advisable to repeat the search in any other record collections in which the same source is included, which may require using a different online search service.

Some parish registers have been indexed by volunteers, who have submitted information to FreeReg. Information for some parishes may also have been submitted to the Online Parish Clerk Project, particularly for counties in the southwest of England. An Online Parish Clerk, not to be confused with a parish clerk, is a volunteer who transcribes genealogical records relating to a particular parish, and may also do lookups and answer enquiries.

Brick walls and errors are more likely to occur when researchers attempt to rely on the contents of incomplete index-only records, without checking whether any further information is included in original sources. An occupation or abode included in a baptism record, for example, could provide a vital clue to a further source. Whenever index-only records or partial transcriptions are identified that appear to be relevant, every effort should be made to consult photographic facsimiles, or when that is not possible to obtain full transcriptions. If it is impracticable to visit archives where original sources are held, or other locations where microfilm copies are available, it is usually possible to pay for copies or transcriptions of specific records to be made.

Collections of browsable digital images of some sources have been made available online without the individual records having been indexed, although it may be possible to locate images of specific records more easily if they can be identified using other search tools, sometimes available through different online search services. TNA has digitized selected sources previously available on microfilm, referred to as 'digital microfilm', which are large files that can be downloaded and viewed on computer. FamilySearch has made available digitized images of some parish registers and other sources, some of which can only be accessed on computers located in LDS family history centres. Essex Record Office has digitized all deposited parish registers for the county, which can be viewed online after paying a subscription. The availability of such digitized sources means that it is no longer necessary to visit relevant archives, but browsing systematically through images is still necessary and may be slower than browsing images on microfilm. Provided that a computer with an adequate specification is being used, the speed of loading of high-resolution images is dependent on the speed of the internet connection. In areas where broadband speeds are low, upgrading to fibre broadband, if it is available locally, can significantly improve the experience of browsing images online.

ONLINE RECORD COLLECTIONS

Online record collections are referred to at the time of writing as:

- Datasets or Record sets (Findmypast)
- Historical record collections (FamilySearch)
- Databases or Record sets (The Genealogist)
- Record collections or Data collections (Ancestry).

Searching all record collections simultaneously using the default search on the main search page, sometimes described as 'search all records' or 'master search', can be a useful first step in identifying records relating to an individual or family, but as explained above multiple results are sometimes obtained for the same historical records if the same source is included in two or more record collections.

When relevant record collections have been identified it is recommended to search them separately, as the search options are usually tailored to the database structure and often include a wider range of search criteria than the default search. Searching record collections covering specific geographical areas can also reduce the number of irrelevant records retrieved. Separate record collections can be found on Findmypast by selecting *A-Z of record sets* and on Ancestry by selecting *Card Catalogue*.

Findmypast: A–Z of record sets.

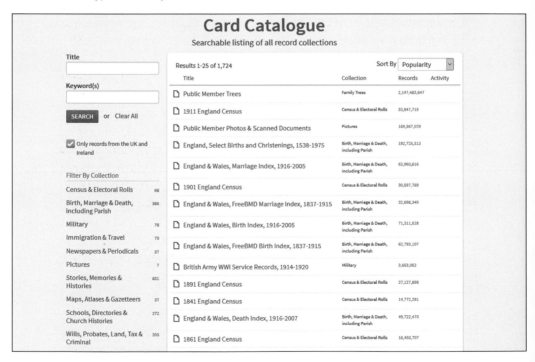

Ancestry: Card Catalogue.

Collections of church registers made available through online search services are usually easy to identify as they have titles such as 'Devon Baptisms' or 'Norfolk Marriages'. The major challenge in using them effectively is to establish exactly what they include or, more significantly, what they don't include.

Record collections produced by local family history societies generally comprise index-only records or full or partial transcriptions, but without links to images, relating to specific counties or parts of counties. They include indexes or transcripts of baptisms, marriages and burials covering specific periods of time, together with other specialist indexes. Indexes or transcripts of baptisms, marriages and burials for some counties are as complete as surviving records will permit, with any deficiencies in parish registers filled using information from bishop's transcripts and other sources. Indexing has usually been carried out by local volunteers who are familiar with local place names and surnames, and information on the date coverage for each parish is usually available.

The content of digitized parish register collections is usually based on the original registers deposited in specific archives in their role as diocesan record offices. The relatively few parish registers for the pre-Victorian period that are still held in churches are unlikely to have been included. Even when deposited in archives, parish registers are still owned by incumbents or parochial church councils and a small number of parishes have refused permission for their registers to be digitized. If original parish registers no longer survive, any printed, typescript or handwritten transcripts now used as substitutes are unlikely to have been digitized. Bishop's transcripts are not necessarily located in the same archive as the corresponding parish registers, and those that are may not have been included in digitization projects. After the digitization of sources at the archive premises, the indexing of records has usually been carried out overseas by people who have been trained to read old handwriting but have no personal familiarity with local place names and surnames. Digitized parish register collections are often released in

117

tranches, and it is not always easy to find accurate information on the parishes included or the date coverage for each parish.

Because the LDS was refused permission to film parish registers in some dioceses, some baptism and marriage records in LDS record collections were produced not from original parish registers, but from printed, typescript or manuscript transcripts or incomplete collections of bishop's transcripts. Most of the LDS index records for Devon baptisms and marriages, for example, are based on transcripts of parish registers, mainly produced before the Second World War, previously held in Exeter Central Library and now at Devon Heritage Centre, which cover only about 60 per cent of Devon parishes.

Effective research using online search services therefore requires establishing which sources are included in relevant online record collections and identifying and searching separately any sources that are not included, which may require visiting the relevant archive or another location where a microfilm copy is available. If earlier parish registers have not survived, or there is a gap, the existence and location of bishop's transcripts should be investigated, and any relevant search tools identified. Parish maps are essential for identifying all the parishes in a particular area.

Pre-1837 Nonconformist and Roman Catholic registers of births, baptisms, deaths and burials deposited with the Registrar General in the nineteenth century and now held at TNA are now searchable online, but some may be held in local archives, as mentioned in Chapter 6.

USING SEARCH TOOLS

The most significant issue for genealogical researchers when using search tools is the variant spelling of names. Until the nineteenth century there was much less standardization in spelling, not only among people who were illiterate or semi-literate, but also to some extent among more educated people. As discussed in Chapter 4, during the pre-Victorian period a relatively small number of Christian names were very common. Problems are therefore more likely to be experienced with surnames, but can also occur with uncommon

Christian names, including surnames used as Christian names, and Christian names that have been abbreviated or recorded in Latin.

Conventional printed indexes usually collate surname variants, but may differ in the way in which this is done. Variants such as Giles and Gyles have sometimes been grouped under a single heading with a *see* reference from the other variant. Surnames may also have been listed exactly as they were recorded in original sources, but with *see also* references to other variants. Even when no attempt has been made to collate surname variants, they can be identified relatively easily in alphabetical indexes by browsing, taking into account any variants that may not begin with the same letter, such as Horrell and Orrell.

Online record collections are structured databases consisting of separate records, each of which corresponds to a historical record. Database records comprise several 'fields' in which text is stored. When information from historical records is transcribed and entered into database records, specific elements are entered into specific fields. The fields in a baptism record, for example, include the parish name, the baptism date, the surname, the Christian name of the child baptized, the father's Christian name and the mother's Christian name. This database structure enables two or more fields to be searched in combination. A record will only be retrieved when names in relevant fields correspond to names entered by the searcher.

Most search systems incorporate a system for the automatic retrieval of name variants. Searchers may be given the choice between 'exact match' and 'variants' and in some cases between 'close variants' and 'all variants'. Automatic matching generally works reasonably well for Christian name variants and for common surname variants, but in some cases too many records containing irrelevant names are retrieved, and in others records containing name variants that have previously been identified are not retrieved at all. Computerized search tools do not necessarily retrieve all the name variants that would otherwise be easily identifiable by researchers browsing systematically through original sources. Some surname variants were specific to certain geographical areas. For example, in some parishes in Co. Durham, variants of the surname Bruce included Brewes, Brewis and Brewhouse, but searching for this surname using the 'all variants' option is unlikely to identify them all. It is therefore advisable to identify all possible variants in advance and to search separately for those that have not been retrieved automatically.

Identification of records containing name variants is therefore dependent not only on understanding how different search tools deal with name variants but also on having identified the full range of possible variants for each name that is being searched for. Browsing systematically through several years of parish registers in areas where surnames were concentrated may enable further name variants to be identified. Browsing through printed transcripts, when they are available, can be a quick method of identifying surname variants, as they can usually be browsed much more quickly than the images of original sources.

Some records containing abbreviated or contracted Christian names may not be retrieved automatically when using online search tools, when this would not be an issue when browsing through images or using alphabetical indexes. As explained in Chapter 4, a name written in a parish register as Jos^h, where the h has been written as a superscript, is an abbreviation for Joseph, and is sometimes transcribed in full or in the form Jos[ep]h. If the name has been entered into a database record simply as Josh, automatic name matching is likely to identify it as a variant of Joshua, so the record would not be found when searching for the name Joseph. Names recorded in Latin have usually been transcribed as they stand, and search systems may or may not have been designed to identify the Latin versions automatically. Online search services such as Ancestry and Findmypast include record collections from a variety of different originators, which may have adopted different procedures for dealing with abbreviated and Latin Christian names.

Computerized search tools generally permit some degree of 'wildcard' searching, in which symbols can be entered as substitutes for one or more letters. A distinction is sometimes made between wildcards and truncation symbols. The term wildcard is sometimes used specifically to refer to a symbol used to replace a single letter, with the symbol used to replace any number of letters, usually at the end of a word, referred to as a truncation symbol. Sometimes both types of symbol are referred to as wildcards. Irrespective of how they are defined, it is common practice in computerized search systems for the question mark (?) to be used to replace a single character and for the asterisk (*) to be used to replace any number of characters. In some search systems * can only be used at the end of a word (right-hand truncation), but in others can also be used at the beginning of a word (left-hand truncation) or in the middle.

When using search tools that allow searching using these symbols, searching for H?yw??d would retrieve records containing the variants Hayward, Heyward, Haywood and Heywood. Searching for Hay* and Hey* would not only retrieve records for these variants, but also for all the other surnames beginning with these two stems. Searching for Jos* would retrieve records in which Jos^h had been entered as Josh, as well as records containing Joseph, Joshua, Josiah and Josephine. The exact implementation of wildcard searching varies from one online search service to another, so it is advisable to consult help pages or search guides before attempting to search for word variants using such symbols.

There may be some ambiguity when dates between 1 January and 24 March before 1752 occur in database records, as different practices may have been adopted for different record collections. Determining whether dates in particular record collections have been converted to 'new style' is not always easy to establish, but in any case, whenever a record of interest is found it is advisable to consult the original source or a photographic facsimile. Quakers did not refer to months by name but by number. Before 1752 'first month' was March not January. The death of George Fox, the founder of the Quakers, was recorded as the 13th day of 11th month 1690, which was not 13 November 1690 but 13 January 1690/1. People indexing Quaker records have not always been aware of this system of dates, and errors have often occurred when the numbered months before 1752 have been incorrectly interpreted.

UNSUCCESSFUL SEARCHES

A negative search result describes a situation in which nothing has been found, but when stating that a search was unsuccessful, it is important to clarify exactly what procedure was followed. Search tools have the potential to enable genealogical information to be retrieved quickly and easily, but they are not infallible. Relevant records that are present in original sources may not be retrieved using search tools for two main reasons:

• Index records contain transcription errors and omissions made during their compilation.
• Searchers have not used appropriate search terms, such as unusual name variants.

Because one or both of these factors could potentially be the reason why a record has not been retrieved, browsing through the section of the source where a record might have been expected may result in it being found, and the reason why it was not automatically retrieved by the search tool discovered. In the majority of cases a record will still not be found, but researchers are now able to state with greater confidence that the search was unsuccessful. In some cases systematic browsing of a source will reveal a plausible explanation of why a record is missing, such as a gap of several months in a church register during which no events were recorded, or an error that was an obvious 'slip of the pen'. It is therefore advisable to browse systematically through relevant sections of original sources whenever records cannot be found in likely sources using search tools.

Systematic browsing may be unavoidable when no search tools are available, but browsing the contents of large sources is only practicable if it is possible to limit the amount of browsing to a specific section, such as range of dates. In some cases relevant records may not be located in the section that has been selected, such as very late baptisms many years later, so may remain inaccessible until search tools eventually become available. Some sources contain several overlapping sequences, and records can be missed if this is not obvious. Guides to sources and descriptions in archive catalogues sometimes highlight such irregularities.

Chapter 9

ARCHIVES AND LIBRARIES

Even though a considerable amount of material for some areas has now been digitized, solving genealogical problems in the pre-Victorian period almost always requires access to some sources that are only available in archives. Library local history collections may also hold unique or rare sources. Using archives and libraries effectively is an important research skill, and requires an understanding of their function and organization and the types of search tool available to enable relevant information to be identified.

LOCAL ARCHIVES

Historical records relating to counties and boroughs, such as Quarter Sessions records, were often stored in designated rooms in official buildings before the twentieth century. County and borough record offices were originally established to preserve such records, but their remit was gradually extended to include other local records. Many local record offices were set up before the Second World War, with others in the post-war period. Before the establishment of record offices, many larger public libraries, established in the nineteenth century, built up manuscript collections relating to their local areas, most of which have subsequently been transferred to local archives.

Although some parish records had previously been deposited in archives and libraries, following the Parochial Registers and Records Measure of 1978 specific archives were designated as diocesan record offices for the deposit of ecclesiastical parish records. Churches were permitted to continue to hold their own historical records only if certain conditions were met, and only a very small proportion chose to do so.

Local archives may hold a range of original sources relevant to genealogical research in the pre-Victorian period, depending on their size and location. Sources available in local archives include:

- parish registers
- parish chest material, including churchwardens' accounts, Poor Law material and vestry minutes
- records of post-1834 Poor Law Unions
- bishop's transcripts
- marriage licence bonds and allegations
- probate records
- church court records
- Nonconformist and Roman Catholic records
- Quarter Sessions and Petty Sessions records
- family, estate and manorial records.

Wiltshire and Swindon History Centre in Chippenham.

The organization of local archive services varies and the geographical areas for which records are held often overlap as a result of historical boundary changes. Cumbria is an example of a county with a decentralized archive service operated by a single local authority, with separate record offices in Carlisle, Kendal, Barrow-in-Furness and Whitehaven. In Yorkshire, historically divided into North, West and East Ridings, reorganization of local authority boundaries has resulted in a number of local archive services containing genealogical sources for the county, and some sources are held at the Borthwick Institute at the University of York. Most boroughs in metropolitan counties (created in 1974 but whose councils were abolished in 1986) provide archive services, either separately or collectively. London Metropolitan Archives covers the whole of the Greater London area and individual boroughs also provide archive services.

The location of original records is often dependent on historical boundaries and subsequent changes that can initially appear perplexing to researchers. As a result of the creation of new dioceses and reorganization of existing dioceses, mainly after 1837, parish registers and bishop's transcripts for the same parish are sometimes located in different archives. For example, because Berkshire was originally in the Diocese of Salisbury but is now in the Diocese of Oxford, bishop's transcripts are held at Wiltshire and Swindon History Centre in Chippenham, which holds the records of the Diocese of Salisbury, whereas parish registers are held at Berkshire Record Office in Reading, which is a diocesan record office for the Diocese of Oxford.

As well as making heavily used material in their own collections available on microfilm, many archive services have also acquired microfilm copies of sources relevant to the area they cover but which are held elsewhere, such as church registers held in neighbouring archives and sources held at TNA. Microfilm copies of pre-1837 Nonconformist and Catholic registers held in local archives are usually copies of original registers held at TNA, which have now been digitized. Microfilming has enabled duplicate sets of parish registers to be made available in more than one location and the location of original parish registers may only be an issue for researchers if sections of microfilm are illegible and access to originals is sought.

Following the separation of ecclesiastical and civil parishes in 1894, ecclesiastical records, including not only parish registers but also other records of parishes in their ecclesiastical role, such as churchwardens' accounts, remained in the ownership of churches. The ownership of records relating to parishes in their civil role, mainly consisting of Poor Law records, passed to parish councils, although in practice many remained in churches, particularly in rural areas. This can result in Poor Law and ecclesiastical records for the same parish being held in different archives. For example, most Poor Law records for parishes on Tyneside and Wearside are held at Tyne and Wear Archives in Newcastle upon Tyne, where local parish registers are also available on microfilm. The original parish registers, however, are held at Durham County Record Office and Northumberland Archives, which are the diocesan record offices for the dioceses of Durham and Newcastle respectively.

In recent years many local authority archive services have been amalgamated with library local history collections, so that original sources and published works relating to the same area are both available in a single location. Library local history collections are discussed later in this chapter.

THE NATIONAL ARCHIVES

The Public Record Office (PRO) was established in 1838 to preserve national records, which had previously been scattered in various locations throughout London. The PRO merged with the Historical Manuscripts Commission in 2003 to form TNA. TNA is located at Kew in southwest London, but lesser-used collections, as well as those that have been digitized, are stored in the DeepStore storage facility at a salt mine in Cheshire. Sources held by TNA that are of particular relevance to genealogical research in the pre-Victorian period include:

- pre-1837 Nonconformist church registers
- probate records of the Prerogative Court of Canterbury
- army service records and muster rolls
- Royal Navy and Royal Marines service records and ships' muster rolls
- records of the Customs and Excise
- records of merchant seamen
- records of the assize courts
- criminal and convict transportation registers
- records of the equity courts (Chancery proceedings)
- records relating to land ownership and taxation.

The National Archives at Kew, in southwest London.

A significant amount of material in some of these categories has now been digitized and made available online, but there remains a large amount of material relevant to genealogical research that has not been digitized. Bevan (2006) is a comprehensive guide to genealogical sources held at TNA and there is also detailed information on TNA's website. TNA also has a large library containing books and periodicals relevant to genealogy and local history for the whole country.

SPECIALIST ARCHIVES

Some major libraries have extensive collections of archives. Collections relevant to genealogical research at the British Library in London include the records of the Honourable East India Company and India Office, and manuscripts from a variety of sources, including collections of family papers.

Some archive services in universities hold original sources that elsewhere are held in local authority archives. The Borthwick Institute at the University of York holds the diocesan records of the Diocese of York, including wills, marriage licence records and bishop's transcripts, together with parish records for the Archdeaconry of York. Durham University Archives and Special Collections holds diocesan records of the Diocese of Durham, including wills, marriage licence records and bishop's transcripts. Cambridge University Library holds marriage licence records and bishop's transcripts of the Diocese of Ely. The University of Nottingham holds marriage licence records of the Archdeaconry of Nottingham. College archives at the universities of Oxford and Cambridge hold records relating to land now or formerly owned by colleges in many different parts of the country, as well as records of former students and fellows. Significant family and estate collections have been deposited in the archives of some universities.

Small specialist archives may also hold sources for researching ancestors with specific backgrounds. Many long-established organizations, including religious denominations, educational institutions and professional bodies, hold collections of archives. The records of some landowning families are still held privately, but many are accessible to researchers. Details of specialist archives can be found using the *Discovery* catalogue, referred to later in this chapter.

USING ARCHIVES

Archives are quite different from libraries, where users can gain an impression of what is available by browsing the shelves. Because the items held in archives are unique and irreplaceable, they are stored in secure areas known as *strongrooms*, usually in boxes or other protective storage, and are directly accessible only to archive staff. Archives resemble retail catalogue showrooms, in which customers use a catalogue to identify the items they require, which are then fetched from storage areas by members of staff. Archive users must identify the items they wish to use, which if not available on microfilm or microfiche are fetched by archive staff, referred to as *producing* items, for use in the reading room or *searchroom*. As well as original sources and microfilm copies, archives also provide some relevant printed and unpublished reference sources, usually in searchrooms where they are directly accessible to users.

The use of catalogues is essential to identify and order specific items. In many archives requested items are fetched only at specific times, so it may be necessary to submit requests well in advance on the day of a visit. Some archive services offer the facility to pre-order items one or more days in advance. Items held at remote storage locations may require several days' advance notice. Major sources for genealogical research that have not been digitized are usually made available in searchrooms in the form of self-service microfilm or microfiche, but it may be necessary to reserve a microfilm reader. The space available for consulting original sources in searchrooms is limited, and some archive services either require or recommend advance bookings to be made.

Visiting an archive premises for the first time can be daunting, even for experienced researchers, as the organization of searchrooms and the procedures for identifying and ordering items are often quite

A storage area at The National Archives. Original records are stored in boxes.

different from one archive service to another. Most archives require users to have a reader's ticket, and require suitable identification before a ticket can be issued. A single ticket provides access to those archives that are members of CARN (County Archives Research Network). Archive staff are usually able to provide a very brief introduction to searchroom arrangement and ordering procedures for new users, but there is often a lot of information to absorb on a first visit, so it is advisable to study relevant archive websites in advance. Many archive services hold annual open days during which they offer tours, including areas behind the scenes not normally accessible to users, and some offer courses on using archives in family history research.

Using archives effectively requires understanding the principles of how they are organized and awareness of the range of catalogues and other search tools available for specific archives to enable relevant items to be identified. As discussed in Chapter 3, the term *records* is used to describe the archival materials of specific record creators or originating bodies. All records had an original day-to-day function, and collections of records recognized as having enduring historical value have been deposited in archives. Unlike in libraries, where books on the same subject are shelved together, each record collection is kept together as a unit, preserving its original arrangement. Similar types of record, such as deeds relating to a single parish, can therefore be scattered in many different record collections.

Identifying relevant sources located in specific archives requires knowledge not only of the range of potential genealogical sources that could be held there but also of changes in boundaries and responsibilities that may affect where sources are now located. Specific information on the location of local sources is available in a series of A5-sized pamphlets, many authored or co-authored by Jeremy Gibson and known as 'Gibson Guides', originally published by the Federation of Family History Societies and now by The Family History Partnership, with titles such as *Probate Jurisdictions: Where to Look for Wills* and *Bishops' Transcripts, Bonds and Allegations: A Guide to their Location and Indexes.* These pamphlets are often available for consultation in libraries and archives. Knowledge of changes in county and diocesan boundaries from the nineteenth century onwards in the area of research can be very helpful in explaining and identifying the current location of sources.

ARCHIVE CATALOGUES

As mentioned in Chapter 3, original sources exist in two main physical formats: bound volumes comprising multiple genealogical records, such as church registers, and collections of individual loose items, each of which is a separate record, such as wills and deeds. Individual records in bound volumes are rarely listed separately in archive catalogues. Whether individual loose items are listed separately is dependent on the depth to which specific record collections have been listed, and is discussed further below.

The identification of individual genealogical records in bound volumes held in archives, such as baptisms, marriages and burials in church registers, usually requires the use of separate search tools, both online and printed, produced by family history societies, various other organizations and individuals. The use of such search tools, when available, may also be necessary when individual items, such as wills and marriage licence documents, have not been listed separately by the archive itself. When relevant record collections have not been listed in sufficient depth and no search tools are available, finding relevant records requires identifying possible sources and browsing their contents systematically, with the possibility that nothing relevant will be found. The various methods by which records in sources held in archives may be identified are shown in Figure 3.

Many archives now provide online catalogues, but the extent to which their existing paper catalogues have been retrospectively converted varies. Some archives have fully converted their paper catalogues, but in many others only a proportion of collections are currently included in their online catalogues.

As well as the online catalogues of specific archives, usually accessible via their websites, a significant amount of material held

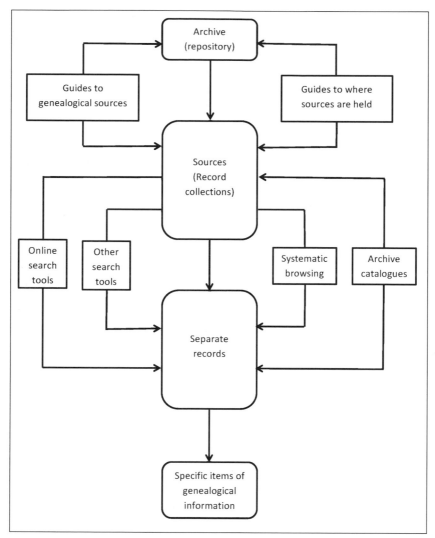

Figure 3: Searching for information in archives.

in many archives can be identified using *Discovery*, a union catalogue of archival material held both at TNA and in a large number of English and Welsh archives. The online catalogue records for collections not located at TNA were originally produced from archives' paper catalogues as part of the *Access to Archives* (A2A) project in the early twenty-first century, when few archives had their own online catalogues. Not all the material held by participating archives was necessarily included and no new catalogue records have been added in recent years. There is now considerable overlap between the contents of Discovery and the online catalogues of many archives, but Discovery remains the only online search tool available for some archives. Discovery also incorporates various other lists that were previously separate, including a directory of archives in the United Kingdom and the Manorial Documents Register. Discovery enables the holdings of multiple archives (that were included in A2A) to be searched simultaneously. A similar union catalogue of archives located in academic institutions is the *Archives Hub*.

Most archives also have supplementary indexes covering specific types of material, some of which may be available via their websites as separate databases or lists. Other indexes may only be accessible at archive premises, such as card indexes of wills or Poor Law documents. Depending on the extent to which paper catalogues have been retrospectively converted into electronic format, searching for information in archives may require using a combination of two or more of the following:

- the archive service's own online catalogue
- Discovery
- paper catalogues and associated name and place card indexes, accessible only at the archive premises
- supplementary indexes to specific types of material, produced by the archive itself
- search tools produced independently of the archive by individuals, record societies and family history societies.

The principles of the organization of archive catalogues are the same whether they are paper-based or computerized. The contents of record collections are listed or *described* in the form of hierarchical inventories corresponding to their physical arrangement, but the depth or *level* to which record collections have been listed varies. A typical hierarchical arrangement of a record collection is shown below, with some of the terms used by archivists to refer to the different levels of description shown in parentheses:

1. Whole record collection (record collection or fonds)
   2. Records of similar type (section, series or sub-fonds)
      3. Box, bundle or volume stored as a single item (file or piece)
         4. Smallest separate item (item)

In large record collections level 2 is often further subdivided. These basic levels of description can be demonstrated in the hierarchical relationship between the records of a specific parish (record collection) and an individual settlement examination (item):

1. Parish records (for a single parish)
   2. Records of the Overseers of the Poor
      3. Bundle of settlement examinations
         4. Settlement examination of a specific person

The levels of description are reflected in the hierarchical systems of letters and numbers used to list and label record collections, which may be referred to as *reference numbers*, *reference codes*, *shelf marks*, *catalogue references* or *document references*. There is no standard system, and some archive services have inherited two or more systems as a result of amalgamation, or started a new system on a specific date. A typical system of reference numbers for parish records is illustrated below:

PR/Dow	Downton parish records
PR/Dow/7	Records of the Overseers of the Poor
PR/Dow/7/4	Settlement examinations, 1694–1832 (67 items)
PR/Dow/7/4/36	Settlement examination of James Woodward, 1787

The listing of each settlement examination as a separate item is an example of the most specific level of description in archive catalogues, referred to as *item level description*. Listing record collections containing large numbers of physically separate items at item level is time-consuming and staff-intensive, and few archives have the resources to catalogue all their collections at this level. Some archive services have been poorly funded compared with others, but external funding has sometimes enabled collections of historical importance to be listed in more detail than would otherwise have been possible.

The level of description of record collections in archive catalogues is particularly relevant when searching for physically separate items, such as Poor Law documents and deeds, which include the names of one or more people. It will only be possible to identify such items by searching for names in archive catalogues if the relevant record collections have been described at item level. Most collections of parish records are likely to be described to least at Level 3 (box, bundle or volume), usually with the date range recorded, and often with an indication of the number of separate items. Whether separate items in collections of parish records (including settlement certificates, settlement examinations, removal orders and bastardy documents) have been listed individually in archive catalogues will vary from one archive service to another, and may also vary between different collections of parish records in a single archive.

Specific categories of record (such as Poor Law documents, marriage licence documents and wills) may not be included in archive catalogues, but may have been listed separately in databases or card indexes, or independently by individuals, record societies and family history societies. Miscellaneous search tools of this type are sometimes referred to as *supplementary finding aids*.

In recent years the depth to which some record collections in archives have been listed has been greatly improved with the assistance of volunteers. Members of the Friends of the National Archives, for example, have contributed to the more detailed cataloguing of many record collections of relevance to genealogical research, such as military records and Chancery proceedings.

The level of description of record collections relating to landowning families in a single archive often varies considerably. In collections of records of landed estates the hierarchical relationship between the collection as a whole and separate deeds might be as follows:

1. Historical records of a landowning family
    2. Deeds
        3. Bundle of deeds relating to one or more parishes or manors
            4. Separate deed naming the parties involved

The names of individuals and families involved in land transactions will only be searchable in archive catalogues if the contents of relevant record collections have been described at item level. In collections not listed in such detail it may only be possible to identify unlisted bundles of deeds relating to specific parishes or manors where families that are the focus of research are known or believed to have lived. Systematic browsing of such bundles may result in relevant deeds being identified, but as with any speculative browsing there is no guarantee that anything will be found.

Unlike traditional library catalogues, which consist of drawers of cards, with each card corresponding to a separate book title, traditional archive catalogues usually consist of descriptive inventories typed on A4 sheets and arranged in binders. Most archives also maintained alphabetical name and place indexes, usually in the form of card indexes, in which all the names and places from the typed catalogue descriptions were included. When archive services created computerized catalogues from the contents of their paper catalogues, all the words became searchable. Computerized catalogue systems therefore enable catalogue records containing a combination of two or more search terms to be identified, which is particularly useful when searching for a surname and place name in combination. Although computerized catalogues offer powerful search facilities when searching for one or more specific terms, there are some potential disadvantages compared to traditional paper catalogues, including the following:

• Online catalogues can be tedious to browse.
• Surname variants may be missed if they are not identified and searched for separately.
• A large number of irrelevant results may be obtained when searching for those surnames that have other meanings.

In traditional paper catalogues, catalogue descriptions for whole record collections are set out over several pages in the form of hierarchical inventories. In the online catalogue systems currently provided by most archives, catalogue records are displayed individually and linked hierarchically in a tree structure, so browsing the contents of record collections often requires navigating through a large number of separate catalogue records. Some archives continue to provide and maintain a paper catalogue in parallel with their online catalogue, so when carrying out research at an archive premises it can often be quicker and easier to use the paper catalogue for browsing.

Unlike database records in online record collections available through genealogical search services, which are subdivided into very specific text fields that can be searched separately and in combination, the catalogue records in archive catalogues are much less structured and more descriptive. Any words of genealogical significance, such as personal names and place names, usually occur in the *title* and *description* fields. A catalogue record is only retrieved when the words entered by the searcher correspond to words in searchable fields, with little or no automatic searching of spelling variants. The spelling of surnames and place names in archive catalogues usually reflects the practice in the corresponding original sources, but conventional spellings may have been added as an aid to searching, particularly for place names, such as Newbourn

[Newburn]. Because names have not been entered into specific fields, they must be searched for as if they were ordinary words. It is therefore advisable to identify all possible surname variants in advance. Researchers interested in the surname Combe will not find catalogue records containing the variant spelling Coombe unless they identify it as a variant and search for it separately. Old-fashioned name indexes on cards collated variant forms of surnames or provided cross-references between them. Some archives have retained their card indexes, although they may no longer be maintained, even though their catalogues have been fully computerized. Consulting an alphabetical name index at the archive premises may sometimes enable further surname variants to be identified.

Searching for some surnames in online archive catalogues can be laborious. A significant proportion of surnames have their origin in place names, such as Bedford and Dudley, and occupations, such as Brewer, Merchant, Draper, Potter, Fuller and Tucker. Other surnames, such as James and George, are also Christian names. Searching for such surnames in online archive catalogues may produce large numbers of irrelevant results, so it may be necessary to browse through a large number of online catalogue records to identify all the occurrences of a surname.

The item-level description of an individual lease usually includes details of the transaction, the property and the parties concerned. A typical catalogue description for a lease is as follows:

> Lease for 99 years or three lives: William Combe, his wife Jane and son Joseph.
> 1. James Timpson of Binfield, Esq.
> 2. William Combe of Oldland, husbandman.
> Dwelling house and garden now in the occupation of James Bunthorne and three acres of arable land in Oldland.
> Rent: 5s per annum.

Researchers interested in families with the surname Combe in Oldland would be able to identify the above item by searching for the surname and place name in combination. The method of searching for combinations of terms varies, but in many online catalogues entering more than one term in the basic search box will result in the retrieval of those catalogue records in which all the terms occur.

Most archive catalogues permit phrase searching, either by selecting an option such as 'words appear together as a phrase' or by entering the relevant phrase in double quotation marks. This can be useful when searching for names in the form of a Christian name followed by a surname, and searching for "William Combe" would enable the above deed to be identified, as this exact string of text occurs in the catalogue record. However, catalogue records are only retrieved when strings of text entered as search terms correspond exactly to strings of text in catalogue records. Searching for "Jane Combe" or "Joseph Combe" would not result in the retrieval of the above catalogue record, even though people with those names are referred to. Some degree of 'wildcard' searching is usually possible in archive catalogues, but may be limited to right-hand truncation, using the asterisk symbol (*) to search for word variations beginning with the same stem.

LIBRARY LOCAL HISTORY COLLECTIONS
Public library services operated by local authorities have always collected books of local interest, and either established separate local history or local studies libraries or built up collections of local material in major libraries. It was, and still is, often necessary for researchers wishing to use a combination of original sources and published materials for the same local area to visit two separate buildings, sometimes several miles apart. In recent years the advantages of amalgamating library local history collections with archive services has been recognized, and many local authorities have established history centres or heritage centres. The majority of the books in local history collections are usually available on the open shelves, but with old and irreplaceable material stored in strongrooms and available on request. Different software is used for

book and archive catalogues, so books in local history collections, whether or not the collection is part of a history or heritage centre, are usually listed in the online catalogue of the relevant public library service.

Sources relevant to genealogical research that may be available in library local history collections include:

• pedigrees
• family histories
• county histories
• local histories
• series of publications, often comprising transcriptions and indexes of historical records, including those published by local record societies, the British Record Society and the Harleian Society.

Many old books that are out of copyright have been digitized, and books originally published in sufficient quantities that copies found their way into major libraries worldwide are often freely available online. Some old books published in more limited quantities have been digitized by individuals and local organizations, and these are often available for purchase on CD or as downloadable files. Many other old books of local interest have not been digitized and may now only be available in library local history collections. Library local history collections also contain many books still within copyright, many of which were published in small quantities and are now out of print.

Library local history collections often include unpublished and semi-published material, some of which may have been produced several decades ago, including:

• parish register transcriptions and indexes
• monumental inscriptions
• manuscript and typescript notes relating to specific families and parishes.

Similar types of material may also have been deposited in archives, so it is advisable to search for such material in both archive and library catalogues.

Library local history collections usually include local newspapers on microfilm, and some local indexes have been produced. An extensive collection of local newspapers is held by the British Library, which is currently being digitized (the *British Newspaper Archive*), providing access to a vast amount of material that was previously only accessible with a definite clue to the date of an event. In the pre-Victorian period family notices for more prosperous families and reports of Assizes and Quarter Sessions giving information about specific trials can often be found in newspapers, but notices of births, deaths and marriages of people from lower-class families were relatively uncommon. It is usually only practicable to search a newspaper on microfilm if either an index is available or the approximate date of an event has already been established.

GENEALOGY LIBRARIES AND FAMILY HISTORY CENTRES

Many local family history societies have set up research centres providing access to a range of indexes and transcripts of sources relevant to the areas they cover, such as monumental inscriptions, some of which may not be available elsewhere.

The largest genealogical library in England is at the SoG in London, which holds an extensive collection of microfilm copies and transcripts of church registers and monumental inscriptions. Printed and unpublished pedigrees, family histories and compilations of genealogical material are also held. Although a considerable amount of unique material held by the Society has now been digitized, and is available online to members, microfilms and transcripts of church registers and other local sources are sometimes the only copies available outside the part of the country to which they relate.

Many original and derivative sources held in archives and libraries have been filmed by the LDS, and some digital images are now available online. Microfilm copies of many other sources are held at the Family History Library in Salt Lake City, Utah, and are listed online in the FamilySearch Catalog. LDS family history centres are located worldwide, with more than fifty in England. Films listed in the FamilySearch Catalog can be ordered and made available for several weeks at local family history centres for a small fee, and some sources that have been digitized by the LDS are only viewable on computers in family history centres. Although most are small, with limited opening hours, local family history centres may offer an alternative method of accessing some resources that would otherwise require visiting archives some distance away. The largest family history centre in England is the London FamilySearch Centre, currently located at TNA, which holds a large number of microfilms of sources from all parts of the British Isles.

For researchers for whom research in London is more practicable than visiting the relevant area of the country where original sources are located, it may be possible to carry out a significant amount of research using a combination of resources available at the SoG and at the London FamilySearch Centre.

Chapter 10

EVIDENCE AND PROOF

The historian Edward Gibbon (1737–1794), who wrote *The Decline and Fall of the Roman Empire*, made an incorrect assumption about the identity of his great-grandfather, which he recorded in his memoirs. His correspondence reveals that he became aware of his error towards the end of his life, but did not have time before his death to correct his memoirs, which were published posthumously containing the uncorrected account. That even an eminent historian can make such an error illustrates that the identification of ancestors must be based on firm evidence, and not on wishful thinking or because someone has been found who seems to fit.

Evidence is information that provides support for a specific conclusion, and the term can be used to refer both to separate items of evidence and to the sum total of evidence. Whether a relationship between two people can be regarded as proved is dependent on the *weight* of total evidence, rather than its quantity. In the absence of sufficient weight of evidence, someone identified as a possible or probable ancestor cannot simply be assumed to 'be' the ancestor.

Proof of genealogical relationships requires evidence from information in original sources combined with relevant external knowledge. The genealogical information recorded in a single source is often insufficient to establish relationships between individuals with certainty in the pre-Victorian period, and it is often necessary to combine information from several sources. Each separate item of information that has been found must be evaluated as evidence according to the following criteria:

- its reliability as a correct record of the event
- the likelihood that it relates to the person who is the focus of research.

A genealogical relationship can only be regarded as proved if it is possible to reach a valid conclusion based on sufficient weight of evidence. The evidence that has been found must be evaluated in combination, taking into account the following:

- the probability of alternative explanations
- resolution of any issues arising from conflicting items of information.

RELIABILITY OF RECORDED INFORMATION AS EVIDENCE

Records contain information that may be used as evidence. The reliability of recorded information is dependent upon the following factors:

- the truthfulness of informants
- the accuracy of information supplied by informants in good faith
- the accuracy with which information was recorded.

There are circumstances in which people deliberately supplied incorrect information about themselves or their families, often when they had something to hide. Because of the stigma of illegitimacy, unmarried mothers sometimes pretended they were married, so a child could have been baptized as William Burroughs, son of John and Sarah Burroughs, when he was actually the son of Sarah Burroughs, a single woman. Sarah may subsequently have told people, including her son, that her husband John had died. Such deception was feasible in populous parishes in towns or cities where the mother's circumstances were not widely known, but is unlikely to have occurred in rural parishes where everyone knew everyone else. Although evidence can sometimes be found that such deception must have occurred, deliberately misleading information supplied in the past frequently results in brick walls in the present that are impossible to overcome.

The reliability of information given in good faith is dependent on the extent of the informant's knowledge or participation, and recorded information can be divided into two categories:

• *Primary information* is information supplied by an informant with direct knowledge of the facts, such as a participant or witness to an event.
• *Secondary information* is information supplied by an informant with only secondary knowledge of the facts, based on what they had heard.

A single record may include both primary and secondary genealogical information. Most of the genealogical information recorded in parish registers is primary information, with the exception of age at death, which was only recorded routinely in burial registers from 1813. A name in a burial record is primary information, provided that the body of the deceased person could be identified with certainty by at least one reliable witness, but a recorded age at death is secondary information. Even when a deceased person believed they knew their own age and had shared this information with others, it may not have been correct, as people are not witnesses to their own birth, and are reliant on what they themselves have been told.

Secondary information is based on what a person heard, or believed they had heard, and is therefore of variable accuracy, with its reliability as evidence dependent on a variety of factors including:

• The interval of time between hearing information and supplying it to others, which could range from several minutes to several decades.
• Whether the informant heard the information directly from a participant or witness to the event, and if not directly, how many times the information had been passed on.
• The informant's defective memory, including forgetting vital

information perceived to be unimportant, or the confusion of two people or events.
• The informant having misunderstood what they had been told, and 'getting hold of the wrong end of the stick'.
• Adults continuing to believe 'tall stories' they had been told in childhood, perhaps to deflect embarrassing questions.

Errors may have been made when verbal information was recorded, through carelessness or ignorance. The accuracy of recorded information is dependent on a range of factors including:

• The interval of time between the event and the recording of the information.
• The ability of informants to read and check what has been recorded. A name incorrectly recorded by a clergyman in a marriage register after 1754, for example, is unlikely to have been noticed at the time if the bride, groom and witnesses were all unable to read.
• Whether the person recording an uncommon surname had previously encountered it, particularly if the informant was unable to spell the name.
• Whether the person recording the information was conscientious or careless. Someone copying information from notes could lose their place, and combine the first part of one record with the second part of the next, leaving out the information in between. An elderly clergyman or parish clerk could have had a failing memory.
• Whether records were checked after being written. Sometimes two or more people signed to confirm that a document or page was a true record.
• Whether the source was a copy made from an earlier source. A Christian name written in a notebook in pencil as Marg^t, as an abbreviation for Margaret, could be copied into a parish register some time later as Mary.

Unintentional errors, or slips of the pen, can sometimes be identified as such. If John and Mary Smith married in 1787 and went on to have children baptized in the same sparsely populated rural parish at regular intervals until 1808, with a gap between 1797 and 1801, and the parents of a child baptized in 1799 were recorded as John and Sarah Smith, and no marriage record for a John Smith to a Sarah can be found in the area, it would be reasonable to conclude that this must have been a slip of the pen. In a more populous urban area with a more mobile population, however, the probability increases that such an isolated baptism record could relate to the child of different parents.

INTERPRETATION OF INFORMATION AS EVIDENCE

Evaluating information as evidence requires the incorporation of relevant external knowledge and the elimination of explanations that are logically impossible, but researchers are inclined to make assumptions based on what they know or think they know. Assumptions can have varying degrees of validity, and may be divided into four categories.

Fundamental assumptions are entirely true, with no possible alternative explanations, and are usually based on scientific principles for which no exceptions have been found, or on logical possibilities and impossibilities, for example:

• Every person has a biological father and mother.
• Every person is present in one place at any one time, and can never be in two places at once.
• One person can only be in two consecutive places if the time interval for travelling between them is sufficient and consistent with the routes and methods of transport available at the time.

Valid assumptions are true in the vast majority of circumstances, but evidence to the contrary may occasionally be found. Valid assumptions include conclusions established by historical demographers based on the analysis of large population samples. For example, that in the eighteenth century women over the age of 45 did not give birth to children, which is true in the vast majority of cases, but very occasional exceptions may be found.

Invalid assumptions are completely untrue, without exception, and may arise because of lack of knowledge. For example, that it was illegal to marry a first cousin, which is untrue.

Unsound assumptions may be valid in some circumstances but not others, so cannot be accepted without adequate evidence. They are often based on failure to consider alternative explanations. For example, that a son-in-law must have been the husband of a daughter (a son-in-law could also have been a step-son).

The interpretation of information as evidence is also dependent on the context. Assumptions about the relationships between people with the same surname that would be valid in a small closed rural parish with a low population density are more likely to be unsound when applied to a large populous parish in a town or city. Invalid and unsound assumptions can be minimized by gradually building up generic external knowledge, acquiring specific external knowledge as necessary, and becoming familiar with relevant terminology, particularly terms whose meanings have changed over time, several of which are mentioned in this book.

PROOF

Genealogy is concerned with biological relationships, but until very recently establishing absolute proof of relationships between people living today and people long since dead was impossible. The only biological relationship that can be proved virtually conclusively is between a child and its mother. In most cases the source of evidence is the mother herself, corroborated by a witness present at the birth. In a very small proportion of cases, such as when the mother died in childbirth or shortly afterwards, her identity might not have been known, as happened with Oliver's mother in *Oliver Twist*. There are also known cases of babies having been accidentally switched in maternity units shortly after birth, and similar errors are likely to have occurred in the past.

Absolute proof of paternity is more difficult to establish as it is dependent on information supplied by the mother and on that information being correct. Some women may have been unwilling to divulge the name of the father, pretended another man was the father, or not known or not been certain of the father's identity, so the name recorded in sources that are generally regarded as accurate and authoritative may not be the name of the biological father. Since genealogy uses recorded information as evidence, it has never been possible to establish absolute proof. DNA analysis now offers the possibility of proving biological relationships scientifically, but its use in genealogical research in the pre-Victorian period is still in its infancy.

Genealogical researchers struggled with the criteria for establishing proof throughout the twentieth century. There are parallels between establishing proof in genealogical research and reaching a verdict in the civil and criminal courts. Attempts have been made to apply legal criteria of proof, such as *balance of probabilities* or *preponderance of evidence* in civil law and *beyond a reasonable doubt* in criminal law, but it was recognized that neither is entirely appropriate in genealogical research. Greater attention has been paid to criteria for proof in the United States than in other anglophone countries, largely as a result of the requirement for documented proof to be submitted in membership applications to lineage societies, such as the General Society of Mayflower Descendants and Daughters of the American Revolution.

In 2000 the Board for Certification of Genealogists in the United States issued the *Genealogical Proof Standard* and the *Genealogical Standards Manual* (Board for Certification of Genealogists, 2000). The *Genealogical Proof Standard* comprises five components:

- reasonably exhaustive research
- complete and accurate source citations
- critical tests of relevant evidence through processes of analysis and correlation
- resolution of conflicting evidence
- soundly reasoned, coherently written conclusion.

A conclusion is regarded as proved only if all five criteria are satisfied, but it is recognized that such proof is never final, and that new evidence may arise in some cases, resulting in a changed conclusion. The Genealogical Proof Standard is concerned with documented proof, requiring the production of a written report capable of convincing others that the conclusion is valid. Although it is important for all researchers to keep records of the sources they have used, it is not strictly necessary for people carrying out personal research to produce written conclusions. Once they have turned their attention elsewhere, however, researchers may gradually forget the analytical processes and external knowledge that contributed to the conclusions of earlier research, so it may be helpful to summarize these at the time for future reference.

Research often stalls at a point where there is insufficient weight of evidence to prove a genealogical relationship to the level required by the Genealogical Proof Standard, but it may still be possible to estimate the probability that a conclusion is valid. In many disciplines the probability that a correct solution to a problem has been found is expressed by *levels of confidence* such as *certain*, *probable* and *possible*, and similar criteria can be applied to the results of genealogical research. Mills (2015) proposes the categories: *certainly*, *probably*, *possibly*, *likely*, *apparently* and *perhaps*, and Anderson (2014) proposes: *almost certain*, *highly probable*, *probable* and *possible*. Since absolute proof in genealogical research is impossible, some researchers prefer the description almost certain rather than certain.

A probable level of confidence applies to many situations in genealogical research in which the evidence suggests that a certain conclusion seems likely, but insufficient information has been found to raise the level of confidence to almost certain. Recognizing that the relationship between two people is only probable but continuing research on earlier generations simply perpetuates any uncertainty. Although it may be possible to link individuals in both earlier and later generations with an almost certain level of confidence, a 'weak link' of this nature means that there is doubt regarding all the earlier ancestry. Tentative conclusions that are only probable can, however, be regarded as hypotheses while further evidence is sought, or while the research is left on the back burner in the hope that newly indexed records will enable further evidence to be found in due course.

RECORDED AGE AS EVIDENCE

The type of secondary information most commonly encountered in genealogical sources is recorded age, and particularly age at death. Recorded age may be completely accurate in some cases and quite inaccurate in others, but since any recorded age had to be credible, was usually of the correct order of magnitude. Researchers who have traced ancestors through the censuses are likely to have found variations in recorded age for some individuals, resulting in a range of possible years of birth. Discrepancies in recorded age can arise for a variety of reasons, including some people having forgotten how old they were or being reluctant to divulge their exact age, different people in the household supplying information on different occasions, or ages being based on incorrect mental calculations or being simply guesses. Discrepancies in census records may also have resulted from errors made by enumerators when copying information from household schedules.

Older children and young adults are more likely to have known their exact ages than elderly people, providing they had been informed of their correct dates of birth. The age of 21 represented the transition to adulthood. For young people in their teens and twenties coming of age would have been an event in the near future or the recent past, but there were no further milestones in later life such as retirement age. People in the pre-Victorian age were not continually being asked their ages and dates of birth as they are today, so it is likely that in time many people forgot exactly how old they were.

People who were able to read and write are more likely to have kept records and known their dates of birth. Middle-class and more prosperous lower-class families sometimes kept records of the dates of births of children in family bibles. People who were illiterate, however, would not have kept records, and may not have remembered exactly when their children had been born, particularly in large families.

153

When an incorrect age for a living person was recorded and can be identified it is not always obvious whether this was the result of deliberate deception or simply ignorance or carelessness. It might be expected that some people would give incorrect ages in particular situations if they thought they could get away with it, such as minors saying they were of full age in order to marry without the permission of their parents. Baptism certificates were required as evidence of age in some circumstances, and although date of birth was not routinely recorded in baptism registers, most children were baptized within the first few days or weeks after birth.

The average lifespan was much shorter than it is today, but a minority of people did survive to a ripe old age, with a few people living well into their nineties, and there are occasional deaths recorded of people aged over 100. If people died in the parish in which they had been born, some clergymen may have verified their ages by searching for the records of their baptisms, but it is likely that most recorded ages of death in burial registers were based entirely on verbal information from family members or other informants. Parents are likely to have known the ages of their children, but sons and daughters may not have known the exact ages of their elderly parents. Discrepancy between actual and recorded age in burial registers is therefore quite common, and a variation of up to 10 per cent would not be unusual. Even after 1837, age at death recorded in civil registration records was based on unverified information provided by informants. Copying errors may also have been made when information was written up in parish registers from rough notebooks.

In the case study in Chapter 2 it was noted that the age of Arthur Keen, buried at Appleby on 22 August 1783, had been recorded as 59, but that all the other evidence indicates he was 53 or 54. The record of his army service indicates that he was aged 50 when awarded a pension on 7 June 1780, so if this is completely accurate he would have been born between June 1729 and June 1730, which corresponds with the baptism date of 21 April 1730 at Hawkshead. As there is evidence that Arthur Keen could write well, he is likely to have known his own age, so the information in the army record is likely to be accurate. Arthur Keen's wife Hannah was still alive at the time of his death and she is likely to have known his age, so there is no reason to suppose that his actual age was not known when his burial was recorded.

A possible explanation for this discrepancy is that his age was originally recorded correctly, but that a copying error was made later. The handwriting in the Appleby St Lawrence parish register indicates that it was almost certainly compiled retrospectively. The corresponding bishop's transcript includes the same information as the parish register but with the additional description of some people, including Arthur Keen, as 'poor'. From 1783 to 1794 there was a tax on the recording of baptisms, marriages and burials in parish registers, but paupers were exempt from paying, and this information was often recorded. The recording of some people as 'poor' only in the bishop's transcript indicates that it could not have been produced by copying directly from the parish register. It therefore seems likely that both were written up, probably around the same time, from an earlier source that no longer survives, such as a notebook, so it is quite possible that an age originally recorded correctly as 53 or 54 could have later been misread as 59, as the two numbers 3 and 4 are those whose shape most closely resembles the number 9.

As mentioned at the beginning of this chapter, solving genealogical problems requires assessing the credibility of each item of information as a correct record and resolving any issues arising from conflicting information. In this case, a copying error resulting from the retrospective compilation of a parish register offers a credible explanation for a single item of conflicting information.

SIGNATURES AS EVIDENCE
Most records used in genealogical research contain information recorded by people in official positions as part of their duties, but some also include relevant signatures. It was normal for a fairly uniform style of handwriting to be taught in the past, so two people

with the same name could have fairly similar signatures. On the other hand, the handwriting of one individual could change gradually over time, so two signatures written several decades apart, such as on a marriage licence bond and a will, could look quite different. Nevertheless, some signatures were sufficiently distinctive that there can be no doubt that two different records relate to the same person. In the pre-Victorian period it can generally be assumed that everyone in upper-class families, most people in middle-class families and some people in lower-class families had learned to read and write. It was the practice in the past to teach reading before writing, so making one's mark was not necessarily an indication of the inability to read. People who had not learned to write fluently might have learned enough to sign their name, and examples can be found where the same person signed their name on one occasion but made their mark on another. The laboured signatures in childlike handwriting found in post-1754 marriage registers demonstrate that signing their name, or even writing anything at all, must have been a rare occurrence for a significant proportion of people in lower-class families. However, examples can be found of people from humble backgrounds whose handwriting, spelling and general fluency of writing was of a very high standard, and of relatively prosperous merchants and yeomen who made their marks.

The comparison of signatures in two records can provide evidence that two or more events must relate to the same person. James Biggs, who lived in Frome in Somerset in the eighteenth century, was married four times. On one occasion he remarried seven days after the burial of his previous wife and on another occasion the interval was twelve days. As the signatures in the relevant records are distinctive there can be no doubt that they all relate to the same person. Although some people could not sign their name and made their marks, the sources most likely to contain signatures include:

• Marriage registers from 1754 may include the signatures of bride, groom and witnesses.
• For marriages that took place by licence both before and after 1754,

marriage allegations include the signature of the groom, sometimes that of the bride, and that of the father or guardian if the bride or groom was under the age of 21. Marriage bonds include signatures of the groom and the bondsman, who was sometimes a relative of the bride or groom.

• Original wills include the signatures of the testator and witnesses. Probate and administration bonds, which often accompany wills and grants of administration, contain the signatures of the executors or administrators.

• Deeds include the signatures of some or all of the parties to the transaction.

Depending on the probate jurisdiction and the time period, there may be two surviving versions of each will: the original will containing the testator's signature or mark and a registered copy, which is a transcription of the will written in a register after it had been proved. Both versions of wills proved at the Prerogative Court of Canterbury exist, but the images that have been available online for several years are of the registered copies. The original wills are held at TNA, and looking at them requires either visiting or ordering copies.

EVIDENCE FROM PUBLISHED FAMILY HISTORIES AND PEDIGREES
Authored works such as family histories and pedigrees have generally been based on a combination of the personal knowledge of the author, papers in the family's possession, and research using original sources, and may also include the author's speculative conclusions. The personal knowledge recorded in older works can potentially be very valuable, as can information extracted from original sources that no longer survive. The main issue for present-day researchers is usually establishing the reliability of individual items of information in such works. Although some publications of this type include source citations, there is often little or no indication of the source of the information, particularly in the case of pedigrees.

The fact that a pedigree is several hundred years old does not

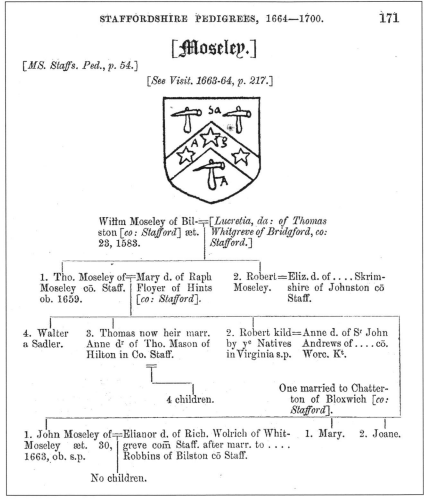

[Moseley.]

[*MS. Staffs. Ped., p. 54.*]

[*See Visit. 1663-64, p. 217.*]

Willm Moseley of Bil-═[*Lucretia, da: of Thomas*
ston [*co: Stafford*] æt. | *Whitgreve of Bridgford, co:*
23, 1583. | *Stafford.*]

1. Tho. Moseley of═Mary d. of Raph   2. Robert═Eliz. d. of . . . . Skrim-
Moseley cō. Staff. | Floyer of Hints   Moseley.   shire of Johnston cō
ob. 1659. | [*co: Stafford*].   Staff.

4. Walter   3. Thomas now heir marr.   2. Robert kild═Anne d. of Sʳ John
a Sadler.   Anne dʳ of Tho. Mason of   by yᵉ Natives Andrews of . . . . cō.
               Hilton in Co. Staff.   in Virginia s.p. Worc. Kᵗ.

                         4 children.   One married to Chatter-
                                              ton of Bloxwich [*co:
                                              Stafford*].

1. John Moseley of═Elianor d. of Rich. Wolrich of Whit-   1. Mary.   2. Joane.
Moseley   æt. 30, | greve cōm Staff. after marr. to . . . .
1663, ob. s.p. | Robbins of Bilston cō Staff.

                    No children.

*A pedigree from a volume published in the early twentieth century based on
information recorded in the seventeenth century.*

provide evidence of its validity. Although unsourced pedigrees
should not be accepted without further verification, they often
contain clues to relationships, such as the maiden names of wives,
which may enable relevant sources to be identified.

Pedigrees of families of landed gentry were recorded by the Heralds of the College of Arms in the sixteenth and seventeenth centuries. The heads of families wishing to use coats of arms were required to produce evidence of their right to do so in the form of pedigrees, but the Heralds varied in the extent to which they sought verification of the information given to them. The information recorded about the parents and probably the grandparents of the person supplying the information is likely to be sound, as it would have been based on personal knowledge, but some siblings of parents or grandparents may have been omitted and the accuracy of earlier generations is likely to vary from one pedigree to another. Pedigrees recorded in the 1660s following the Restoration of the monarchy are particularly valuable in bridging the gap from 1642 to 1660 when record keeping was disrupted as a result of the Civil War and Commonwealth.

Copies of original pedigrees recorded by the Heralds were often made, with information subsequently added from other sources, and it was often these copies, rather than the original pedigrees recorded by the Heralds, that were used as the basis of *Heralds' Visitations* published during the late nineteenth and early twentieth centuries. It can generally be assumed that published pedigrees of this type provide reliable evidence of one or two generations of an ancestral line at the time of a visitation, but the accuracy of information on earlier generations will vary.

Chapter 11

FAMILY RECONSTITUTION

It is often possible to trace an ancestral line back to 1837 without paying a great deal of attention to the siblings of direct ancestors, although it is normal practice to make a record of those who can be easily identified, particularly in census records. New GRO birth indexes introduced in 2016, which now include the mother's maiden surname, have made it much easier to identify siblings, particularly those who were born and died between censuses or were not at their parents' home on census night. However, it is still necessary to purchase certificates to access the full information in civil registration records, so post-1837 baptism and burial records, if they can easily be identified, can often be used as partial substitutes.

Building up a picture of a whole family becomes much more important in the pre-Victorian period because of the minimal information in church registers and the greater potential for ambiguity. Since the 1960s historians and historical demographers have used family reconstitution to group the populations of parishes into family units using information in parish registers. This technique has been used successfully in rural parishes with settled populations, and has been employed in the study of topics such as infant mortality, life expectancy, average age at marriage and fertility. Academic researchers are usually interested in the reconstitution of all the families in a single parish, or group of contiguous parishes, but genealogical researchers may be able to employ a similar technique to compile family trees linking all the individuals with the same surname in a small area, providing evidence of relationships between them. Family reconstitution techniques in genealogical research, including examples from both the Victorian and pre-Victorian period, are discussed in Todd (2015).

Church registers usually provide the basic building blocks for family reconstitution, and in some cases it may be possible to obtain sufficient evidence of relationships between individuals of different generations from church registers alone. In other cases a tentative family tree can be constructed using church registers, but corroborating evidence must be found in other sources. Successful family reconstitution using church registers in a single parish or group of contiguous parishes requires the correlation of the baptisms, marriages and burials for each individual. Family reconstitution is more likely to be successful in the following circumstances:

• The parish or parishes were closed rather than open, so the population remained relatively stable over several generations.
• Parish registers recorded more information rather than less, particularly before 1813.
• The family had an uncommon surname, uncommon Christian names were given, and naming patterns were followed.
• Only a small number of children were born in each generation or survived to adulthood.

The recording of the place of abode in parish registers, more common in larger parishes in the north of England, may also enable distinct family groups to be identified. Even in those pre-1813 baptism registers in which abode was recorded but the mother's Christian name was not, it may still be possible to identify children with the same father's name as belonging to different family groups. For example, if children of two men named Thomas Emmerson were being baptized around the same time it may be possible to group them into separate families if descriptions were used consistently, such as 'child of Thomas Emmerson of Bushblades' and 'child of Thomas Emmerson of Clough Dene'.

Men with the same name but of different ages living in the same parish at the same time were sometimes described in records as 'senior' and 'junior'. As demonstrated in Chapter 13, it cannot be assumed that these terms were always used to refer to a father and son, but this was their most usual meaning in parish registers. Such descriptions are rarely found in parish registers in which only minimal information was recorded, but in those registers that recorded slightly more detail these descriptions can be very useful in family reconstitution, often providing a link between two generations. In some cases the name of the father of someone born in the late eighteenth or early nineteenth century and who married before 1837 can be established if they remarried after 1837.

Age at death was routinely recorded in burial registers from 1813 and earlier in some areas, so family reconstitution based entirely on records in parish registers is more likely to be feasible in the period after the mid-eighteenth century when it is often possible to calculate the approximate year of birth from a recorded age at death. Family reconstitution is less feasible in those parishes in which only minimal details were recorded in parish registers, as there is more scope for ambiguity. In burial registers in which only names and not relationships were recorded, it may be impossible to confirm whether a burial record relates to a child who died in infancy, a young adult, or someone of riper years.

When carrying out family reconstitution in a single parish, a marriage may not be found there because it took place in the bride's parish, as was the common practice, and it was also common for the first child to be baptized there. Establishing the dates of baptism of all the siblings of a direct ancestor can enable the date of the parents' marriage to be estimated. If Robert Wilson, the son of John and Mary Wilson, was baptized in 1825, his parents could potentially have married between 1800 and 1825. Establishing that children were baptized at regular intervals from 1809 to 1831 suggests that the marriage is likely to have taken place around 1808.

Establishing the age and date of death of a married woman or widow can often enable the date of a marriage to be estimated. If the mother of a child born in 1815 died at the age of 62 in 1854, she would have been born about 1792. Although marriages of young women aged 16 and 17 did take place, they were relatively uncommon, so the most likely date of marriage in this case would be between 1810 and 1815.

Identifying a birth record and obtaining a birth certificate for a younger sibling born after the introduction of civil registration in 1837 can enable the maiden surname of the mother of an older sibling to be established or confirmed.

More detailed baptism registers were kept in some areas in the late eighteenth and early nineteenth centuries. As well as 'Dade' and 'Barrington' registers, mentioned in Chapter 7, the maiden names of mothers were also recorded in the baptism registers of some other parishes during the same period, particularly in the dioceses of Carlisle, Chester, Norwich and Salisbury. It is only necessary to find one baptism record of this type for an identifiable sibling to establish or confirm the mother's maiden surname. In some cases records of this type enable the baptism of a sibling in a totally unexpected area to be identified, as in the following example.

George Boaler was baptized at Cuckney in Nottinghamshire in 1823, son of William and Jane Boaler. Several children of William Boaler, a gamekeeper employed by the Duke of Portland at Welbeck Abbey, and his wife Jane, were baptized at Cuckney in the period from 1812 to 1830. William Boaler had been baptized at Cuckney in 1783, but his marriage to Jane could not be found. The isolated baptism of Joseph, son of William and Jane Boaler, was found at Eglingham in Northumberland in 1809, some 180 miles further north. The combination of date, parents' Christian names and uncommon surname suggested that this could be an earlier child. It was possible to confirm that it was because the baptism was recorded during the period from 1798 to 1812, when 'Barrington' registers were kept in parishes in the Diocese of Durham. The baptism record for Joseph Boaler is as follows:

Baptized 20 April 1809, born 6 March 1809, Joseph Boaler of Bewick Nursery. 1st Child of Wm & Jane Boaler of the same

Place. He born in the vicinity of Welbeck, Nots, & Gamekeeper to Wm Sadliere Bruere Esq the present High Sheriff for the County. And she the eldest Daughter of Walter Gray, Gardiner & Farmer at Bewick Nursery aforesaid.

There can be no doubt that the parents of the child baptized at Eglingham in Northumberland were the same William and Jane Boaler who went on to have children baptized at Cuckney in Nottinghamshire. Although the direct ancestor of interest was George Boaler baptized in 1823, the isolated baptism record for a sibling in Northumberland in 1809 is the only source of information that has been found to record his mother's maiden surname as Gray. Identifying both the maiden surname and the name of Jane's father is of particular relevance in this case, because the marriage of William Boaler and Jane Gray has not been found, and may have been an irregular marriage performed just over the Scottish border, for which few records survive.

Witnesses to post-1754 marriages were not always family members, but identifying those who were may enable further sources to be identified. A marriage witness could be a church official, such as the parish clerk or a churchwarden, a friend or a relative. The identity of witnesses who were church officials can usually be established by browsing through the relevant marriage register, as it was common practice for the same people to act as witnesses on a regular basis. A witness with a different surname from the bride and groom may have been just a friend, but could also have been a close relative such as a brother- or sister-in-law. Investigating the witnesses to the marriages of a whole generation of siblings or possible siblings may enable clues to family relationships to be found. For marriages that took place by licence both before and after 1754, bonds and allegations may provide further information about other family members as well as the bride and groom. Marriage bonds were signed by two men, usually the groom and a relative or friend from the same social class. A bondsman with a different surname from the bride and groom could still have been a relative such as a brother-in-law. Since most marriages by licence were between people who were reasonably prosperous, identifying the will of a bondsman or witness, possibly several decades later, may result in relevant genealogical information being found.

More complex family reconstitution can sometimes lead to the solution of genealogical problems. This involves extending the search for family members to a wider area and attempting to trace each sibling from birth to death, including identifying the marriages of females and their deaths or burials under their married names, as well as the deaths or burials of husbands and wives. Tracing people forward in time is not always straightforward, but is usually easier when people stayed in the same area or had uncommon surnames. The increasing availability of online search tools means that tracing siblings forward in time is becoming more practicable. Identifying a sibling who was alive at the time of the 1851 census may enable the birthplace of a direct ancestor to be established who was born in the late eighteenth or early nineteenth century but had died or left the country before 1851.

Civil registration death records in England and Wales are of little genealogical value in comparison with those of many other countries, particularly for adult males. Much more genealogical information was recorded in death records in Scotland and places to which people from England emigrated, including Australia, Canada and some states in the United States of America. In Scotland, where civil registration was introduced in 1855, death records include the father's name and the mother's maiden name, although this information could only be recorded if it was known to the informant. The death record for an identifiable sibling who died outside England during the second half of the nineteenth century may include information to enable the names of both parents of someone born in the late eighteenth or early nineteenth century, but who remained in England, to be established or confirmed.

The will of the elderly sibling of a direct ancestor, or their husband or wife, may include a great deal of relevant genealogical information. Elderly bachelors, spinsters and childless widows and widowers sometimes left legacies to a large number of nephews and nieces, as in the following example.

James Castle died at Stokesley, in the North Riding of Yorkshire, in 1803. He was a childless widower aged 75 who had outlived all his siblings. In his will, proved at the Prerogative Court of York, as well as several beneficiaries specifically referred to as relatives of his late wife, he named a large number of descendants of his own siblings, as follows:

> Henry Appleton husband of my late niece Elizabeth Appleton
> James Wright, Mary Wright, Elizabeth Wright, Jane Wright, Ann Wright and Sarah Wright children of my niece Elizabeth Wright wife of George Wright of West Auckland
> The children of my niece Mary Goundry wife of John Goundry of West Auckland
> The children of my niece Ann Owen wife of George Owen of West Auckland
> John Storer, William Storer and Elizabeth Storer children of my niece Sarah now the wife of Ralph Suddick of West Auckland by her late husband John Storer deceased
> The children of my niece Jane Bradley wife of William Bradley of Stockton
> George Ward, Robert Ward and James Ward, sons of my late Brother in Law George Ward of Wossall

Identifying the wills of siblings or other family members who moved to London can sometimes enable genealogical problems in other parts of the country to be solved. As mentioned in Chapter 6, boys from all over the country were apprenticed in a wide range of crafts and professions in London, but people were also drawn there by a variety of other employment opportunities. The majority of people who died in London had not been born there, and those who prospered may have named family members living elsewhere in the country in their wills. For example, James Castle's brother, John Castle, became a tobacconist in London, and also died childless. His

166

will was proved at the Prerogative Court of Canterbury (PCC) in 1786, and he also left legacies to a large number of nephews and nieces in the north of England.

Soldiers and sailors often made wills before leaving the country, which were subsequently proved if they died overseas or at sea. Most wills proved at the PCC, particularly before the nineteenth century, were those of people from the middle and upper classes, but wills of many soldiers and sailors were also proved there. The wills of soldiers and sailors, not only of direct ancestors but also of their brothers, may enable genealogical problems relating to lower-class families to be solved. George Keen, baptized at Appleby in Westmorland in 1764, son of Arthur Keen who was the subject of the case study in Chapter 2, enlisted in the Royal Artillery in 1786 and made his will in 1802 while serving at the Cape of Good Hope, which was proved at the PCC in 1803. As well as his wife Jane, he named his sister Elizabeth Gibbons in his will. Elizabeth Keen had married William Gibbons in Sunderland, Co. Durham, in 1784, where the couple subsequently lived and children were born. Elizabeth Keen's place of birth was recorded as Appleby in Westmorland in the 'Barrington' baptism records of some of her children, as mentioned in Chapter 7, but if this information had not been recorded it would still have been possible to establish her place of birth by piecing together several items of information from separate sources, as follows:

• Elizabeth Gibbons was buried at Sunderland in 1824, aged 59, but her baptism as Elizabeth Keen could not be found there.
• Several baptisms of individuals named Elizabeth Keen were identified around 1765 using online search tools, of which the nearest to Sunderland was at Appleby in Westmorland, some 65 miles away, on 2 January 1766.
• This Elizabeth Keen had a brother named George baptized in 1764. A record in the *Discovery* catalogue indicates that George Keen, born at Appleby, enlisted in the Royal Artillery in 1786. (The original source at TNA, which has not been digitized at the time of writing,

contains further information, including the fact that George Keen enlisted at the age of 22, so had been born about 1764, and died on 4 November 1802 at the Cape of Good Hope. However, viewing the actual record was not essential to the solution of this genealogical problem, as it was possible to establish that the various records related to the same individual without this further information.)

• The *Discovery* catalogue lists the 'Will of George Keen, Corporal in Captain William Skyring's Company Royal Artillery of Cape Good Hope' proved at the PCC in 1803.

• In this will, which has been digitized and can be viewed online, George Keen referred to 'my affectionate and well beloved sister Elizabeth Gibbons'.

Finding a person who is the focus of research mentioned in the will of another person, usually a relative, whose surname has not yet been identified as being of significance, is usually dependent on the availability of indexes. For example, if baptism records for several children of John and Mary Denton have been found but their marriage cannot be traced, Mary's maiden surname is unknown. If Mary's father, James Anderson, had left a will in which he referred to 'my daughter Mary the wife of John Denton', it would only be possible to identify it if the names mentioned in the will had been indexed. Indexes to the names mentioned in wills have been produced for some probate courts, usually by individuals or local family history societies, and further indexes are in preparation. Some indexes contain only the names of beneficiaries, but others include the names of executors and witnesses.

In the absence of indexes to people mentioned in wills it may sometimes be possible to solve genealogical problems by reading through all the wills of the people who died in one or more relevant parishes during a specific period of time. This is dependent on the availability of search tools that enable wills to be identified by place, and is only feasible if the number of wills is relatively small, so is more applicable to sparsely populated rural parishes. Such speculative searching is more likely to produce results when researching middle-class families for whom there is a higher probability that wills exist.

Deeds, relating to the purchase or rental of property, may also include genealogical information. Most land in England is now registered with the Land Registry. Once land has been registered the retention of original deeds is no longer required for legal purposes, so deeds have either been disposed of or preserved as historical records. Many collections of old deeds have been deposited in archives, but whether deeds survive relating to a family that is the focus of research is largely a matter of luck. Deeds are large documents full of legal jargon, and many include little or no genealogical information, but some contain a great deal, summarizing previous events, transactions, wills and previous deeds. Such information is usually found in *recital* clauses in which each significant fact is preceded by the word 'whereas' written in large letters, for example:

> *Whereas* Robert Wheatley died on the fourth day of August one thousand seven hundred and seventy two intestate leaving him surviving four children namely Ralph, William, Mary (now the wife of James Hilliard) and Jane (now the wife of Simon Copson).
> And *whereas* the said Ralph Wheatley died on the twenty third day of April one thousand seven hundred and seventy six without leaving any issue living at his decease.

As mentioned in Chapter 9, separate deeds may be identifiable using archive catalogues if the relevant collections have been listed at item level, but others may be in collections for which only bundles of deeds have been listed. Finding unlisted deeds requires identifying any collections of deeds relating to the area in which a family is known to have lived and browsing through them individually. Further information about deeds can be found in Alcock (2001) and Wormleighton (2012).

The descriptions of family relationships recorded in some wills and deeds, when combined with information from church registers, can sometimes enable a family tree of several generations to be constructed. People from middle-class backgrounds engaged in disputes with other family members in the civil courts more frequently than might be expected. Chancery proceedings frequently describe disputes over land or property going back several generations in great detail, including describing genealogical relationships and recording the dates of relevant events, so can sometimes enable an extensive family tree to be constructed even in the complete absence of church records.

Chapter 12

MISSING ANCESTORS

The apparent sudden appearance of an individual in the records of a specific area or parish is not necessarily an indication of relocation from elsewhere, as there are many reasons why people cannot be found in the records of the places where their ancestors lived. Some individuals also seem to disappear without trace, and expected marriages cannot be found. It is possible that no records exist because records made at the time no longer survive, events were not recorded, or some events did not take place. It may be difficult or impossible to identify some records because information was recorded incorrectly. Some events may have taken place far away from the usual parish of residence, or overseas. Some of the reasons why births, baptisms, marriages, deaths and burials cannot be found, together with possible solutions, are discussed in this chapter.

MISSING BIRTHS AND BAPTISMS

In the pre-Victorian period baptism was regarded not only as a necessary religious event, but also as a social occasion when the birth of a child was acknowledged and celebrated. Infant baptism was the normal practice in most denominations, but only adult believers were baptized in Baptist congregations and Quakers did not practise baptism. Baptisms were recorded in parish registers and in registers kept by Nonconformist denominations. Births of the children of members were recorded by Quakers and sometimes by Baptists. The survival of parish registers varies, and those for a few parishes only survive from the late eighteenth or early nineteenth centuries. Deficiencies in parish registers can often be filled by bishop's transcripts, but the extent to which they survive and are complete varies from one diocese to another. The survival of Nonconformist records varies considerably. As a general rule the proportion of births and baptisms that can be found in church registers decreases with each previous generation.

Although the survival rate of church registers increases after the mid-eighteenth century, some children appear not to have been baptized during this period, particularly those from lower-class families living in industrial parishes and in towns and cities. From 1783 to 1794 there was a duty of 3d (3 old pence) on baptisms, marriages and burials recorded in parish registers, although paupers were exempt. Marriages continued to take place, as did burials, because bodies still had to be buried, so these events were recorded as before, but some parents seem not to have had children baptized during this period, and may not have bothered afterwards either.

Children not baptized in infancy were sometimes baptized later. A late baptism, not necessarily in the same parish, can often be identified as such, because either the date of birth or age at baptism was recorded. People were occasionally baptized as adults, as in the following example from Lanivet in Cornwall:

3 September 1796 Maria Thomasina daughter of Richard and Bridget Sim, aged 37 years

Several late baptisms of children of Thomas and Sarah Vile, ranging in age from 12 to 20, were recorded at South Petherton in Somerset in 1825 and 1828:

3 April 1825	William (born 6 February 1805)
12 March 1828	Martha (born 13 April 1809)
12 March 1828	Mary Ann (born 24 June 1811)
4 May 1828	Robert (born 3 May 1814)
4 May 1828	Samuel (born 10 June 1816)

Late baptisms were also recorded in Nonconformist registers. The following adult baptism was recorded in the register of births and baptisms at Paul Street Independent Chapel in Taunton in Somerset:

2 January 1818 Ann the daughter of Thomas and Hannah Brewer of the Parish of Bampton, Devon, born 12th May 1794

Thomas Brewer married Hannah Short at Bampton in 1788, but there is no trace of any subsequent baptisms of children in the parish registers of the surrounding area.

With the exception of the baptism of a couple's first child, which often took place in the bride's home parish, if a baptism record cannot be found in the parish where all the other siblings were baptized, and no evidence can be found of any temporary absence, it is likely that the baptism took place there but was not recorded. Nancy Wright married Thomas Corbin at Fawley, Hampshire, in 1807 and died in 1852 with a recorded age of 66. Her place of birth was recorded in the 1851 census as Fawley, so a baptism would be expected about 1786, but could not be found in any of the parishes in the area. Edward Wright, a mariner, married Jane Young in 1776, and the only baptisms for the surname Wright at Fawley in the period from 1781 to 1793 were the children of this couple, but with a gap between Mary in 1784 and Sally in 1791. The Fawley baptism register for this period gives an impression of neglect, suggesting that some events may not have been recorded. The most probable explanation is that Nancy was the daughter of Edward and Jane Wright, and confirmation of this relationship was found in the will of Edward Wright, proved at the Prerogative Court of Canterbury in 1804.

A baptism record may exist but cannot be found because an error was made when the event was recorded. A church register may give the impression that it had been neglected at the time, and sometimes it is obvious that some records must have been written in later. In other cases, it appears that the records for several months or years must have been written up retrospectively by the same person at the same time. The handwriting may be quite neat, giving an illusion of accuracy and completeness, but an apparently well-kept register compiled retrospectively from rough notes of varying degrees of legibility and completeness is likely to suffer from copying errors and omissions.

In the settlement examination of Abraham Everett senior, mentioned in Chapter 7, he said that he had been born in Corscombe in Dorset, and from the age he gave his estimated year of birth was 1761. No record of the baptism of Abraham Everett was recorded at Corscombe, but the baptism of an Arthur Everett was recorded in 1761. The handwriting in the baptism register suggests that several years of baptisms must have been written up retrospectively in the mid-1760s. No other evidence of anyone named Arthur Everett could be found in the area, so it is almost certain that this record relates to Abraham Everett. The error is likely to have occurred when the name Abraham, recorded correctly in a notebook, was misread as Arthur when the parish register was being written up.

Edward and Mary Curtis married at Wincanton in Somerset in 1773 and baptisms of children were recorded from 1773 to 1790, with a gap between Edward in 1775 and James in 1779. The expected baptism of William Curtis could not be found about 1777, but the baptism of William the son of Edward and Mary Cross was recorded the same year. The immediately preceding record in the baptism register is Edward the son of Robert and Mary Cross, and the handwriting suggests that several months of baptisms had been written up retrospectively. No evidence of a couple called Edward and Mary Cross could be found in the area, so it is almost certain that Cross had been written instead of Curtis when the parish register was being written up.

The traditional approach to searching for baptism records, before the widespread availability of search tools, involved searching the baptism registers of parishes in an ever-increasing radius around the parish where an individual or family is known to have lived at a later date. In sparsely populated areas this would sometimes reveal an obvious baptism in a parish a few miles away, as in the example given in Chapter 6, in which children of John and Elizabeth Castle were baptized in five different parishes within a 10-mile radius over a period of twenty years. Although many baptism indexes are now available, they are not necessarily complete. If parish registers have not survived for a parish for the relevant period, bishop's transcripts may be available, and it is important to ensure that they have been searched when necessary to fill in any gaps.

If no baptism records for an individual or any possible siblings can be found in parish registers, it is possible that the family were Nonconformists. It is important to identify any Nonconformist congregations in the area and establish the survival and location of registers. As mentioned in Chapter 6, pre-1837 Nonconformist registers held at TNA have been digitized and are searchable online. Nonconformist registers that were not surrendered in the nineteenth century remained in the custody of churches, but most have now been deposited in local archives. Some Nonconformist registers held by local archives have been transcribed and indexed, often by local family history societies, but others remain unindexed. Pre-1837 Nonconformist registers held locally may sometimes contain the solutions to genealogical problems, as demonstrated in the following example.

Frances Drybrough married Ralph Henderson in 1801 at Newcastle upon Tyne. In the 1851 census she was listed as a widow aged 80, so would have been born about 1770, and her place of birth was recorded as North Shields in Northumberland, within the parish of Tynemouth. Frances's baptism could not be found in the Tynemouth parish register or in any of the local Nonconformist registers held at TNA and now searchable online. However, records of Howard Street Presbyterian Church, North Shields, were deposited at Tyne and Wear Archives in the 1990s, including a baptism register from 1759 to 1779, for which no transcripts or indexes have been produced. A search of this register revealed the baptism of Frances Drybrough in 1770, daughter of Henry Drybrough, a mariner, and his wife Ann.

Even when no baptism records can be found for a whole generation of siblings, often as a result of Nonconformity but sometimes because of defective Church of England records, it may still be possible to establish the identity of the parents, particularly in middle-class families, as in the following example.

Elizabeth Bayly of Westbury in Wiltshire married Bryan Edwards in 1742, and died in 1803, aged 85, so she would have been born about 1718. Elizabeth Bayly also had six known siblings, identified from wills and other sources, but no baptism records for any of them could be found. No relevant wills or grants of administration for the surname Bayly could be found in any of the Wiltshire probate courts, nor any wills proved at the Prerogative Court of Canterbury (PCC). PCC administrations were not searched initially, as they are not searchable online.

Naming patterns in subsequent generations suggested that Elizabeth's father's name is likely to have been Zachary. Although Zachary was not a particularly common Christian name in England at that time, there was a profusion of men named Zachary Bayly in parishes near the Somerset–Wiltshire border, including two men named Zachary Bayly from Westbury, both of whom married women named Elizabeth. The first Zachary Bayly married Elizabeth Lee in 1715 and the second Zachary Bayly married Elizabeth Stephens in 1718, but no subsequent baptisms of children of these couples could be found in the area.

It seemed possible, if not probable, that Elizabeth Bayly was the daughter of one of these men. A search was therefore made for wills for the maiden surnames of their spouses, Lee and Stephens, and the will of Peter Lee of Warminster was identified, proved at Salisbury in 1744. Peter Lee was Elizabeth Bayly's maternal grandfather, and named Elizabeth and all her siblings in his will. This will proves that Elizabeth Bayly was the daughter of Zachary Bayly and Elizabeth Lee who had married in 1715.

Although they are likely to be digitized eventually, at the time of writing PCC administrations are not available online. Identifying a grant of administration requires using a variety of printed, typescript and manuscript search tools, and involves either visiting TNA or paying a record searcher. If an entry of interest is found in an index, the corresponding record must then be located on microfilm. Searching the index for the relevant period revealed a grant of administration for the estate of Zachary Bayly in 1738. Administration was granted to Peter Lee, Zachary Bayly's principal creditor, and the record in the Administration Act Book lists all Zachary Bayly's children by name. Although such a large amount of genealogical information in an administration record is rare, if PCC administrations had been available online it would have been possible to identify this record at an earlier stage.

Two separate sources had therefore been found confirming that Elizabeth Bayly was the daughter of Zachary Bayly and Elizabeth Lee, and it had also been established that Elizabeth Lee was the daughter of Peter Lee of Warminster. This information enabled a dispute in the Court of Chancery in 1738 to be identified. The dispute was between Peter Lee and Mary Bayly, a first cousin of Zachary Bayly, and related to land held by earlier generations of the Bayly family in Westbury. The legal documents produced in connection with this dispute include a considerable amount of genealogical information, and enabled two earlier generations of the Bayly ancestral line to be identified.

Evidence was also found that Peter Lee was a member of an Independent congregation in Warminster, a few miles from Westbury, so the reason no baptism records for children of Zachary and Elizabeth Bayly could be found is almost certainly that the family were Nonconformists. Nonconformity was very strong in this area, but no records of Nonconformist congregations in Westbury survive until towards the end of the eighteenth century. This example demonstrates that it may still be possible to identify several earlier generations of an ancestral line even when the baptisms of a whole generation of siblings cannot be found.

A change of name, usually during childhood, may explain why some baptisms cannot be found. The surnames of some children may have been changed to that of their stepfather after the marriage or remarriage of their mother. Evidence of a change of name can sometimes be found in the continuing use of an alias, and a name by which a person had previously been known was sometimes referred to in legal documents such as wills and deeds. Otherwise, changes of name without formality during childhood are likely to result in brick walls that are impossible to overcome.

If the marital status of a bride who was a widow was not recorded, searching for her name as recorded in the marriage register will result in either no baptism being found or an incorrect baptism being identified. Finding the baptism record of a woman who married as a widow requires identifying that she was a widow at the time of the marriage, identifying the earlier marriage or marriages, if more than one, and then searching for her baptism under her maiden name. Marital status was supposed to be recorded in marriage registers from 1754 but was often omitted, and was recorded inconsistently before 1754. When a marriage took place by licence, both before and after 1754, the marital status of the bride and groom was usually recorded in the bond or allegation. After 1754 marital status was occasionally recorded in banns registers when not recorded in marriage registers, and examples can be found where the banns register of the parish where the marriage did not take place is the only source in which marital status was recorded.

The survival of marriage bonds and allegations and banns registers varies, but as they may contain additional information or clues it is advisable to examine those that survive for the pre-Victorian period as a matter of course. This is particularly important if there is a possibility that the bride might have been a widow but there is no indication of marital status in the marriage register. It may be possible to calculate the age at which a woman married from her age at death. Although the probability that a bride was a widow increased with age, because deaths of young adults and rapid remarriages were both relatively common, some widows were only in their early twenties or sometimes even their late teens when they married for a second time. When not recorded in marriage records, evidence that a woman was a widow when she married can sometimes be found in other sources, such as wills, deeds or Poor Law documents.

Ann Jones, daughter of John and Olive Jones, was baptized at Hereford in 1790. Her parents had married there in 1789, and their names were recorded in the marriage register as John Jones and Olive Meredith, with no indication of marital status. The marriage had taken place by licence, and the marriage allegation recorded that Olive Meredith was a widow. Her first marriage was then identified by searching for the marriage of a man with the surname Meredith to a woman with the Christian name Olive. It was found that Olive Thomas had married John Meredith at Yarkhill, a few miles from Hereford, in 1783. Establishing Olive's maiden surname as Thomas, together with evidence from wills of family members, enabled her baptism to be identified.

MISSING MARRIAGES

From 1754, as a result of Hardwicke's Marriage Act, marriages were normally recorded at the time they took place, when the bride, groom, clergyman and witnesses all signed the register or made their marks. All marriages, apart from those of Jews and Quakers, had to take place in the Church of England between 1754 and 1837, and even when the original marriage register has not survived, bishop's transcripts are more likely to be available for this period. Because such a high proportion of marriage records have survived, failure to identify marriages after 1754 is more likely to be the result of incorrectly recorded information or marriages having taken place at unexpected locations. From 1754 marriages were only supposed to take place in the parish in which either the bride or groom had been resident for a period of four weeks, unless a special licence had been issued. The Faculty Office of the Archbishop of Canterbury could issue special licences to enable marriages to take place anywhere, but these were expensive and only issued in exceptional circumstances. The parishes of residence recorded in marriage registers relate to the parishes where the bride and groom had been living immediately prior to the marriage. 'Of the parish of' or 'of this parish' are not necessarily indications of the permanent parish of residence. A temporary resident was sometimes referred to as a 'sojourner'.

The requirements relating to residence and the calling of banns in the parishes of both bride and groom seem to have been frequently ignored after 1754 by people living in parishes in the vicinity of towns and cities, and some clergymen may also have turned a blind eye to irregular practices. Having banns called in two parishes was double the cost of having them called in only one. The anonymity of towns and cities enabled couples wishing to marry there to say they were both residents and for the banns to be called without any attention being drawn to the fact that one or both of them did not actually live there. Many examples can be found of marriages in urban parishes between couples supposedly 'of this parish' but who were actually from parishes in the surrounding area, although in some cases the bride may have been employed as a domestic servant in the town or city before the marriage.

It was fairly common for couples from the parish of Whickham, an industrial parish on the south bank of the River Tyne in Co. Durham, to marry at the parish of St John, Newcastle upon Tyne, a few miles away, with both bride and groom recorded as being 'of this parish', but with all subsequent baptisms of children taking place at Whickham. Similar patterns can be found in other areas near large towns and cities. George Cross was baptized at Lympsham in Somerset in 1774 and Elizabeth Gould at the neighbouring parish of Bleadon in 1777. They married at St Paul, Bristol, some 20 miles further north, in 1803. Both bride and groom were recorded as being 'of this parish', but it seems unlikely that George Cross had ever lived in Bristol, although it is possible that Elizabeth Gould had been employed there before the marriage. Children of George and Elizabeth Cross were subsequently baptized at Lympsham between 1803 and 1818.

It is sometimes obvious that marriages must have taken place away from the home parish to avoid drawing attention to embarrassing circumstances, such as when the bride was visibly pregnant or the couple already had a child born before the marriage. Thomas Bruce and Elizabeth Smith were unmarried when their daughter Mary was born at Whickham in Co. Durham in March 1819. Mary was baptized at Whickham the following month as Mary Bruce, as though her parents were already married. Thomas and Elizabeth subsequently married in August 1819 at South Shields, some 10 miles away, both recorded as being 'of this parish'. Their next child was baptized at Whickham in August 1821. It seems unlikely that Thomas and Elizabeth ever lived in South Shields, but married there to avoid drawing attention to their situation.

There appears to be little evidence of unmarried couples living together openly as man and wife in the pre-Victorian period. At a time when divorce was virtually impossible to obtain, some couples in which one or both partners were already married may have cohabited, but to avoid social disapproval may have started a new life in a new area where they were not known and it was assumed that they were married. Such circumstances may explain the failure to find some marriages and be the cause of some brick walls. Middle-class men sometimes fathered children by lower-class women whom they had engaged as housekeepers or servants. Examples can be found where the offspring of such relationships were given a middle-class upbringing and education, and sometimes took the father's surname, but without their parents ever marrying.

Banns registers were kept from 1754, but not all have survived. Banns were supposed to be called in the parishes of both bride and groom, and finding a record of the calling of banns in a parish where one of the parties is known to have lived can sometimes enable the parish where the marriage took place to be identified. This can be particularly useful if the bride and groom had been living in different counties before the marriage.

Searching indexes of marriage licence bonds and allegations can sometimes enable the location of elusive marriages to be established, but the availability of indexes for different areas varies, not all are searchable online, some indexes are only available in the repository where the original records are held, and some may not have been indexed at all.

Identifying a marriage in a completely different part of the country may be dependent on establishing a logical and plausible connection between two areas. As mentioned in the previous section, Frances Drybrough, daughter of Henry and Ann Drybrough, was baptized in a Nonconformist church in North Shields in

Northumberland in 1770, and the baptisms of three siblings were also identified. No marriage could be traced in the northeast of England, but the marriage of Henry Drybrough and Ann Hills was found in 1763 at Shadwell in Middlesex, some 300 miles away. In the vast majority of cases a marriage at such a distance from the area where baptisms were recorded would be an indication of two completely different families, but in this instance there is a logical connection between the two areas. At that time coal mined in parishes along the banks of the River Tyne was carried to the mouth of the river in boats where it was loaded into sea-going ships, many of whose crews lived in North Shields. Much of the coal mined in the area was destined for London, where it was unloaded at Wapping and Shadwell. North Shields and Shadwell were therefore at opposite ends of a regular shipping route. Henry Drybrough was described as a mariner in the baptism records of his children, and living in North Shields is likely to have been involved in the London coal trade. The Shadwell marriage record indicates that the marriage took place by banns, and both bride and groom were 'of this parish'. Drybrough is a locative surname of Scottish origin, which was sufficiently uncommon outside Scotland at that time that the probability of two men named Henry Drybrough both marrying women named Ann within the space of a few years outside Scotland is very low. Not only could no marriage be found in the northeast of England, but no baptisms of children could be found in the London area. The level of confidence that the marriage in Shadwell relates to the couple whose children were born at North Shields can therefore be estimated as probable. Both bride and groom signed the Shadwell marriage register, so a matching signature for Henry Drybrough in a document relating to the Tynemouth area would provide conclusive evidence of this connection.

Failure to find marriage records before 1754 is more likely to be the result of missing or defective marriage registers. Because there was no requirement to sign the register on the day of the marriage, some marriage registers appear to have been written up some time later, and some marriages that took place may not have been recorded. No records of the calling of banns were kept before 1754, but records relating to marriage licences have usually survived in diocesan records and may enable some marriages to be identified. When bonds and allegations have not survived, it may be possible to find records of the issue of licences in marriage licence registers or act books. Although marriages did not always take place following the issue of a licence, if children were subsequently baptized it is almost certain that a marriage occurred. Baptisms of children of John and Elizabeth Capron were recorded from 1736 at Cruwys Morchard in Devon but no record of their marriage could be found in parish registers. A bond dated 1 November 1735 survives for the marriage of John Capron and Elizabeth Marwood, both of Cruwys Morchard, confirming that the marriage almost certainly took place shortly afterwards.

Before 1754 it was fairly common for middle- and upper-class couples to marry by licence some distance away from their home parish, often in towns or cities. Marriage licences could be issued not only by the diocesan authorities but also by designated clergymen known as surrogates. Marriages by licence frequently took place in churches where the clergyman was a surrogate and able to both issue a licence and perform the marriage ceremony, usually on consecutive days but sometimes on the same day. Some churches were particularly popular, and a marriage in a town or city within a 20-mile radius of the normal parish of residence was not uncommon, as in the following examples:

> Martin Shepherd and Martha Collins, both of Marston Magna in Somerset, married at St John, Glastonbury, some 15 miles away, in 1701.
> John Thurman and Elizabeth Healy of Grendon in Warwickshire, in the Diocese of Lichfield, married at Lichfield Cathedral, some 15 miles away, in 1725.
> Peter Hodges and Sarah Chamberlain, both of Stretton Grandison in Herefordshire, married at Hereford Cathedral, some 10 miles away, in 1745.

Irregular or 'clandestine' marriages also took place before 1754 in locations such as the Fleet Prison in London, but these came to an end in 1754 as a result of Hardwicke's Marriage Act. Marriage in front of witnesses was legal in Scotland, so couples from England could make a brief visit there in order to marry. Marriages took place not only at Gretna Green, but at several other locations just over the Scottish border, such as Coldstream Bridge and Lamberton Toll near Berwick-upon-Tweed. Marriages between runaway couples from all parts of England took place in these locations, but they were also popular with people living in English parishes near the Scottish border. Many couples from Berwick-upon-Tweed married at Lamberton Toll, which was within walking distance of the town. The surviving records of such 'irregular border marriages' are fragmentary, and further information can be found on the National Records of Scotland website.

Marriage settlements were often drawn up in advance of marriages between people from the middle and upper classes. As they almost always concerned the conveyance of land, marriage settlements are often found in bundles of deeds, and it may be possible to identify them in archive catalogues when relevant collections have been catalogued at item level. Although they do not include details of the location of the marriage or its exact date, marriage settlements often include genealogical information, such as the name of the bride's parents. Ralph Edge married Jane Saunders, probably in September 1719, and they subsequently lived in Strelley, Nottinghamshire, where several children were baptized. No record of the marriage has been found, but a marriage settlement has survived in the 'Edge of Strelley' collection at Nottinghamshire Archives. The relevant parties to the marriage settlement, dated 3 September 1719, were Ralph Edge, William Saunders of Sutton Coldfield, Warwickshire, gent., and his youngest daughter, Jane Saunders, by his wife Margaret. As well as providing evidence of the marriage between Ralph Edge and Jane Saunders, this marriage settlement also includes the additional genealogical information that Jane was the youngest daughter of William and Margaret Saunders of Sutton Coldfield.

Newspaper marriage announcements became common towards

the end of eighteenth century. Most were for upper-class couples, some were for middle-class couples and a few were for more prosperous lower-class couples. Many newspapers can now be searched online, so the marriages of people away from their home areas can sometimes be identified. For example, the *Newcastle Courant* of 2 August 1800 recorded the following marriage:

On Monday se'nnight, at Liverpool, Mr Robson, tin-plate-worker, of Hexham [Northumberland] to Miss Edge, confectioner, of the former place.

Missing Deaths and Burials

The identification of deaths and burials is usually less critical to solving genealogical problems than the identification of baptisms and marriages, but death and burial information can be of significance in family reconstitution, particularly if the age of the deceased person was recorded or can be established from other sources such as a monumental inscription. Establishing the place and date of burial may also enable wills to be identified more easily. Age was only routinely recorded in burial registers from 1813, but from that date only the name, abode and age of the deceased person were usually recorded, with no genealogical information such as the name of a child's parents or a woman's husband. Such information had previously been recorded in some burial registers, and clergymen in a small number of parishes continued to record this information after 1813. Because of the limited information recorded in burial registers both before and after 1813 it is not always possible to associate a burial record with a specific person in the absence of corroborating evidence such as a will or monumental inscription.

Everyone who died on land had to be buried. With the exception of those Nonconformists who were buried in the churchyards of their own denominations, the vast majority of people were buried in a parish churchyard or one of the relatively few cemeteries that were established in the pre-Victorian period. Failure to find a burial record is likely to be because the burial either took place in the parish of residence but was not recorded, or took place in an unexpected location. It was normal practice for burials to take place within a few days of death, and burials in the churchyards of parishes where deaths occurred usually took place within two to three days.

It was quite common for an elderly widow or widower to move to another parish to live with the family of one of their children, usually nearby but sometimes some distance away. When they died it was common practice for their body to be transported back to the parish where they had previously lived to be buried in the same grave as their deceased spouse. Sometimes a body was transported to a parish many miles away to be buried in a family grave, with the burial taking place up to a week after death. Whether a body was transported to another parish for burial is likely to have depended on the distance involved, the ability of the family to pay for transport and the cause of death. Young adults were sometimes buried in a family grave with their parents, and if they were married their surviving spouse would often be buried elsewhere, particularly if they remarried. The failure to find a burial record for a widow may be because she had remarried and was buried under a different name.

The burials of Nonconformists will not be found if their church had its own burial ground and the burial registers have not survived. However, monumental inscriptions may have been recorded and some for the pre-Victorian period may still be legible. A Baptist church was established in Wellington in Somerset in the late seventeenth century, but birth and burial records only survive from the late eighteenth century and are incomplete. A church minute book, commencing in 1723, includes the names of church members at various times. Many of the people listed can be identified in the Wellington parish church marriage register, but no records of their births or burials have survived.

People from middle- and upper-class backgrounds who could afford to travel and workers involved in the transport of people, animals and goods sometimes died while on a journey away from home. Claud Johnson, a Birmingham merchant, died in 1802 and the following year his widow Mary died while visiting Neston, a parish on the Wirral in Cheshire some 100 miles away, and was buried there on 25 September 1803. She was recorded in the burial register as 'Mary Johnson from Birmingham'. The purpose of her visit to Cheshire is unknown and it is only because her death had been recorded in family papers that the location of her death and burial could be established.

From the late eighteenth century death notices of people from middle-class backgrounds were more likely to appear in newspapers, which can enable deaths in unexpected locations to be identified. No record of the death of Elizabeth, the wife of Richard Wilkins, a linen draper of Lawrence Lane in London, could be found, until the British Newspaper Archive became available and a death notice in the *Bath Chronicle & Weekly Gazette* revealed that she had died at Sidmouth in Devon in 1829:

17 Jul 1829 died at Sidmouth, after a lingering illness, Elizabeth, wife of Richard Wilkins, late of Lawrence Lane.

Accidental deaths of people from all social classes were often reported in newspapers. The *Bath Chronicle & Weekly Gazette* dated 11 February 1762 reported:

Friday last Francis Wiltshire, Driver to one of Mr. James's Bristol Stage-Wagons, coming from Marlborough to Chippenham, had the Misfortune to fall as he was driving the Waggon, by which Accident the Wheel went over his Head and kill'd him on the Spot. He had followed that Business 30 Years, and has left a Wife and nine Children.

Wills of people who died abroad were proved at the Prerogative Court of Canterbury (PCC), which also issued grants of administration when people died overseas without leaving wills. The place of residence often appears in indexes as 'Pts', meaning 'foreign parts'. Although images of the registered copies of PCC wills have been available online for several years, as mentioned earlier in this chapter administrations have not been digitized at the time of writing. PCC grants of probate and administration include those for soldiers and sailors who died abroad, as well as people from more prosperous backgrounds. Grants of administration contain less genealogical detail than wills, but sometimes contain important clues.

The dates and places of death of merchant seaman who died overseas or at sea can sometimes be established from records of charities that provided financial assistance to their widows and families, including national organizations such as Trinity House and local charities such as Trafalgar Square Aged Seamen's Homes in Sunderland. Details of these organizations can be found in guides to researching merchant seamen. The records sometimes include genealogical information, including dates and places of birth and marriage. Newspaper reports from the late eighteenth century onwards may also enable deaths at sea of merchant seamen to be traced, particularly captains of ships (master mariners). For example, the *Newcastle Courant* of 12 November 1803 reported:

> The Nile of South Shields Capt. William Wintrip, is lost in the East [Baltic] Sea, crew saved, but the master is since dead from fatigue and cold.

Chapter 13

MISTAKEN IDENTITY

Because of the minimal genealogical information in many records of the pre-Victorian period, researchers are more likely to make unsound assumptions and associate incorrect records with specific people than in the period after 1837. In the past, people who were interested in their own ancestry may have made similar errors for similar reasons, so pedigrees and family stories should not be accepted just because they are old. Unsound assumptions and common errors are discussed in this chapter.

UNSOUND ASSUMPTIONS

There are many assumptions that are true in the majority of cases but not all. Errors can therefore arise when researchers make assumptions that are generally true but are untrue in particular instances. Unsound assumptions can also result when the meaning of words has not been understood in the context of the records in which they appear. Examples of unsound assumptions include:

• A man's wife or widow was the mother of his children.
• Two men with the same name referred to as 'the elder' and 'the younger' or 'senior' and 'junior' were father and son.
• A bride or groom recorded as being 'of this parish' had been born in the parish.
• The absence of information on marital status in a marriage record implies that the bride or groom was unmarried.

Unsound assumptions based on the content of wills include:

- A man who left everything to his wife had no surviving children.
- A testator who named several children had no other living children.
- A man who referred to his 'present wife' or 'now wife' had been married previously.
- A son-in-law was the husband of a daughter.
- A brother or sister was a biological sibling.
- A cousin was the son or daughter of an aunt and uncle.

The term 'son-in-law' had a broader meaning than it does today and could refer to a step-son. Someone referred to as a 'brother' or 'sister' could be a brother-in-law or sister-in-law, or a half-sibling or step-sibling. The term 'cousin' could refer to almost any relation by blood or marriage.

The relationship between people who were almost certainly related was not always stated explicitly in records, and it can be easy to jump to conclusions based on the most likely explanation without considering other possibilities. A household in Co. Durham in the 1841 census consisted of the following three people with the same surname:

William Hodgson	(60) [i.e. 60–64]	not born in county
Jane Hodgson	(45) [i.e. 45–49]	born in county
Sarah Hodgson	(20) [i.e. 20–24]	not born in county

Although it is the most likely explanation, the assumption that this household must represent a father, mother and daughter, or father, stepmother and daughter, is unsound, and in this example is incorrect. The actual relationship in this case is that Sarah was William's niece, and had the same surname as her uncle because she was the illegitimate daughter of his sister, who had died in 1836. Both William and Sarah had been born in Cumberland and had moved to Co. Durham during the 1820s. William and Jane married in 1838, only three years before the census, and neither had been married before.

Terms that are still in use today but whose meaning has changed can lead to the incorrect interpretation of information. 'Son-in-law' and 'cousin' have already been mentioned. Before the eighteenth century the term 'nephew' (from the Latin 'nepos' meaning grandson) often referred to a grandson, and at that time a nephew in the modern sense would often be referred to as a 'cousin'. As mentioned in Chapter 5, before the mid-eighteenth century 'Mrs' was an indication of social rather than marital status, so could refer to an unmarried woman. In the legal sense an 'infant' was anyone under the age of 21 and an 'orphan' was a child whose father had died, so the mother could still have been alive. The term 'friends' was sometimes used to refer to anyone not acting in an official capacity, including members of a person's own family.

The description of two people with the same name, usually men, as 'senior' and 'junior' or 'the elder' and 'the younger' enabled two people of different ages living in the same parish to be distinguished in records, but this did not necessarily imply that they were father and son. In most cases two men described as 'senior' and 'junior' in parish registers were father and son, and it may be possible to confirm this relationship by family reconstitution, but two men distinguished in this way in some other types of source could have been uncle and nephew, first cousins, more distantly related, or not related. In the following example two men of the same name living in the same parish referred to in a deed as 'the elder' and 'junior' were apparently not related at all.

Evidence from a variety of sources indicates that there were two men of similar age named Thomas Wilkins living in Brackley in Northamptonshire in the late eighteenth century: one was an attorney who married in 1751 and died in 1798, and was the father of several children, including a son named Thomas born in 1757, and the other was an innholder who married in 1762 and died childless in 1804. The evidence indicates that Thomas Wilkins the attorney had been born at Brackley and Thomas Wilkins the innholder at Middleton Cheney a few miles away, but no common ancestor has been identified. A series of deeds held at

Northamptonshire Record Office relating to the Crown Inn in Brackley includes a conveyance dated 1803 between Thomas Wilkins the elder of Brackley, gent., and Thomas Wilkins junior of Brackley, printer and innkeeper. Conclusive evidence exists to prove that Thomas Wilkins junior was the son of Thomas Wilkins the attorney, who had died in 1798, so the man referred to as Thomas Wilkins the elder named in the deed could not be his father. The conveyance of an inn in a small town between two men with the same name but who were not related seems unlikely, but the evidence indicates that this must have been the case.

Unsound assumptions can be made regarding age at marriage, which in most cases was not recorded in the pre-Victorian period. Although the majority of first marriages occurred when both bride and groom were in their twenties, a first marriage could take place at any age, as in the example of William and Jane Hodgson, mentioned earlier in this chapter, who married for the first time aged 57 and 43 respectively. Men rarely married before the age of 21, but slightly earlier first marriages became more common towards the end of the eighteenth century, particularly among men from lower-class backgrounds. Marriages of men aged 16–18 were rare, but marriages of women of such an age, who were usually marrying older men, were not uncommon among all social classes. Deaths in early adulthood could lead to the remarriage of a widow or widower at a relatively young age. Remarriage after a relatively short period of time was not uncommon, often after a year or two but sometimes only a few weeks after the death of a previous spouse, and occasionally after only a few days. Some people remarried three or four times. Marriages were legally permitted between certain relations, such as first cousins and step-siblings, but marriages between some relations not related by blood were legally prohibited. Although a man was prohibited from marrying his deceased wife's sister, and a woman from marrying her deceased husband's brother, such marriages did occur and seem to have gone largely unnoticed by the authorities.

INCORRECT ASSOCIATION OF RECORDS WITH PEOPLE

A major challenge in genealogical research, particularly in the pre-Victorian period, involves establishing whether a record that has been found for a person of the same name relates to the person who is the focus of research. A further challenge involves establishing whether two or more records in different sources for the same name relate to the same person. The probability that a record that has been found in the same area and seems to fit the person who is the focus of research actually relates to someone else is increased in the following circumstances:

- The surname was common in the area.
- The Christian name was also common.
- Some parish registers are known to be missing or defective.
- Nonconformity was common.
- The area had a large and mobile population.

Several different types of error can occur when researchers make assumptions in the absence of sufficient evidence:

- Assuming there was only one person when there were actually two.
- Assuming there were two people when there was only one.
- Correctly identifying that there were two people, but associating incorrect records with the person who is the focus of research.

The first type of error often arises because of the fragmentary nature of surviving records, and it is relatively easy to jump to such a conclusion when few records have been found that seem to fit together. The second type of error is more likely to be made when there were significant changes in a person's circumstances, such as remarriage or a change of occupation, giving the illusion of two people of the same name. A man could remarry later in life to a much younger woman and have a second family, giving the impression that there were two men who could have been father and son. A blacksmith could have become an innkeeper, and an agricultural labourer could have become a coal miner and then a quarryman, but it is inconceivable that a surgeon or lawyer would have become an agricultural labourer, or vice versa.

Before the widespread availability of indexes to church registers, searching for baptisms, marriages and burials involved systematically browsing through the pages of parish registers in an ever-increasing radius around the parish where an individual or family is known to have lived at a later date. Browsing through pages of records enables explanations for the absence of events, particularly baptisms, to be easily identified, such as periods during which few or no events were recorded. Errors of mistaken identity are more likely to be made when relying on search tools and not examining original sources, and can be reduced by systematically browsing those sources where expected records cannot be found to seek possible explanations. If a baptism record cannot be found in an expected parish, this does not necessarily imply that the baptism record of a person of the same name in a nearby parish around the same time must relate to the person who is the focus of research, because there may be other more plausible explanations, as in the following example.

Ann Sly married Thomas Stratford at Colesbourne in Gloucestershire in 1797. Ann died in 1855 at the recorded age of 82, and her place of birth was recorded in the 1851 census as Colesbourne, so a baptism record would have been expected to be found there about 1773. However, the only baptism that could be found for an Ann Sly in the area around that time took place in 1769 at South Cerney, some 10 miles from Colesbourne. This is a few years earlier than expected, but falls within an acceptable range for a year of birth calculated from the age at death of an elderly person from a lower-class background. It would be easy to conclude that this must be the correct baptism simply because it was the only one that could be found in a parish not too far away from the recorded place of birth, but examination of the Colesbourne baptism register provides an alternative and more plausible explanation. Children of Joseph and Mary Sly were baptized at Colesbourne at regular intervals between 1760 and 1781, with an average interval of two years between baptisms, but with a gap between Samuel in 1770 and Mary in 1775. An average of six baptisms took place at Colesbourne each year, but only two were recorded between August 1773 and July 1775, so it is almost certain that some baptisms took place during this period but were not recorded in the parish register. It therefore seems probable that Ann Sly had been born at Colesbourne during this period, as recorded in the census, and not at South Cerney.

Information can sometimes be found to prove that a particular record could not possibly relate to the person who is the focus of research, such as finding a burial record indicating that a child whose baptism record has been found did not survive to adulthood. If two possible baptism records have been found, and one burial record for a child of the same name, it may be possible to eliminate one baptism record as a possibility if some other identifying factor, such as the father's name, or the names of both parents, or the place of abode, was included in the burial record, as in the following example:

23 October 1791	John the son of William and Mary Burgon was baptized
25 March 1793	John the son of John and Elizabeth Burgon was baptized
7 October 1797	John the son of John and Elizabeth Burgon was buried

If the baptism of John Burgon who married in 1815 is being sought around 1792, and the name of his father is not known, the burial record in 1797 confirms that the John Burgon baptized in 1793 did not survive to adulthood. Although the remaining baptism in 1791 may well relate to the John Burgon who is the focus of research, this should not necessarily be assumed. A process of elimination resulting in only one record remaining does not in itself prove that this record relates to the person who is the focus of research. Making inappropriate assumptions without considering the likelihood of alternative explanations may to lead to an incorrect association between records and people. Without corroborating evidence, the level of confidence that a baptism record relates to a person of that name who is the focus of research is dependent on a variety of factors discussed in previous chapters. It is sometimes possible to prove that a record that has been found does not relate to the person who is the focus of research, as in the following example.

Children of Thomas Gibbons, a cooper, and his wife Elizabeth were born at Morland in Westmorland between 1723 and 1733, and evidence suggests that their marriage took place at Greystoke in Cumberland, some 12 miles away, in 1723. The only baptism record for an individual named Thomas Gibbons that could be found in the area was at Greystoke in 1704, the son of the rector of Greystoke, also named Thomas Gibbons. The baptism record includes the exact date of birth, a few days before the baptism, so if the birth and marriage at Greystoke related to the same person, he would have married at the age of 18, which is unlikely but not impossible, as William Shakespeare had been only 18 when he married the 26-year-old Anne Hathaway. The Reverend Thomas Gibbons died in 1716, and it is conceivable that the younger son of a clergyman might have subsequently slid down the social scale after being apprenticed as a cooper following his father's untimely death. It was possible to find evidence that Thomas Gibbons who married at Greystoke could not possibly have been the son of the rector. The most significant item of evidence was the will of Hester Acton, paternal grandmother of Thomas Gibbons, the son of the rector, made in 1718 and proved at the Prerogative Court of Canterbury in 1721, in which he was left a substantial legacy, sufficient to enable a lower-class family to live in relative luxury. Identification of this will involved research on the ancestry of the Reverend Thomas Gibbons, including establishing that his father Matthew Gibbons, a London linen draper, had died at a relatively young age and his mother Hester subsequently married Richard Acton, the son of a baronet.

Although it has not been possible to establish the ancestry of Thomas Gibbons the cooper, sufficient sources exist to enable the paternal ancestors of the other Thomas Gibbons, born in 1704 into a middle-class family, to be traced back through several previous generations.

PAST MISTAKES

Errors of mistaken identity also occurred in the past when people who were interested in their own ancestry made assumptions based on insufficient evidence or wishful thinking. People who are not particularly interested in their family history often know very little about the origins of their grandparents, particularly if they never knew them, and in the past, when life expectancy was much lower, many people are likely to have known even less. The following example relates to a case of mistaken identity that originated in the eighteenth century.

James Davenport (1750–1841) was Vicar of Stratford upon Avon in Warwickshire for over fifty years. He was the son of William Davenport (1713–1798) of Reading in Berkshire, an ironmonger who became sufficiently prosperous that four of his sons were able to attend the University of Oxford, all of whom became clergymen. All the families with the surname Davenport living in Reading in the eighteenth century were descended from James Davenport's grandfather, another William Davenport, who married Grace Alloway at Swallowfield, near Reading, in 1707. James Davenport believed that his grandfather had been born at Worfield in Shropshire in 1680 into a family of minor gentry. This account of his ancestry was known to the friend who wrote the obituary that appeared in a local newspaper after his death, which explained his descent from the Shropshire family.

James Davenport's descendants were therefore convinced that this account must be true, despite the subsequent discovery that an individual named William Davenport had been baptized at Reading in 1682. In the early twentieth century one descendant carried out a great deal of research to try to prove William Davenport's ancestry, but the evidence he found was inconclusive. More recent research has revealed a grant of administration in the Berkshire Archdeaconry Court confirming that William Davenport's mother, Elizabeth, died at Reading in 1712, whereas the mother of the William Davenport born at Worfield, also named Elizabeth, had died there in 1709. This grant of administration is the key item of evidence proving that William Davenport of Reading could not have been the individual born at Worfield in 1680.

William Davenport died in 1723 leaving a young family and his widow remarried three years later, so it is likely that his descendants knew very little about his origins. Later in the eighteenth century one or more descendants may have become interested in William Davenport's origins and made enquiries at the College of Arms. A pedigree of the Shropshire family may have been found, which included an individual named William Davenport born about the right time. Davenport is a locative surname that originates in Cheshire, where it was still largely concentrated at that time. The Reading family may have assumed that their surname was much rarer than it actually was, and concluded that this William Davenport must be their ancestor.

Following the discovery of the grant of administration mentioned above, the evidence now suggests that William Davenport was baptized at Reading in 1682, son of Lawrence and Elizabeth Davenport, and that Lawrence Davenport may have been born in Cheshire and served an apprenticeship in London. Until recently, the ancestry of William Davenport was only of interest to some of his own descendants, but because one of them is Catherine Elizabeth (Kate) Middleton, now Duchess of Cambridge, he has become an ancestor of an heir to the throne. In the early twentieth century the unproven Shropshire ancestry of William Davenport found its way into a published family history. A century later this information was discovered by journalists and accepted as factual without further verification, leading to articles in the popular press describing spurious connections between supposed distant ancestors of the Duke and Duchess of Cambridge.

This example illustrates that assumptions about the identity of ancestors based on insufficient evidence occurred in the past as well as occurring in the present, so any pedigrees or information passed down through families should not be accepted at face value just because they are old, but verified by carrying out research in original sources.

ERRORS IN PUBLISHED WORKS

Rather than being based on sound genealogical research using original sources, many published pedigrees and biographical directories contain information supplied by families themselves or extracted from other printed sources. *Burke's Landed Gentry* was first published in 1826 (the first edition was entitled *A Genealogical and Heraldic History of the Commoners of Great Britain and Ireland*) and several subsequent editions have been published. Pedigrees have been mainly supplied by the families themselves, and many people from middle-class backgrounds are included who married into the families listed. The accuracy of early pedigrees may be suspect for the reasons outlined in Chapter 10, but there may also be errors in the information recorded for more recent generations. Such an error appears in the pedigree of the Edge of Strelley family relating to the Reverend James Davenport, who married Margaret Webb, daughter of John Webb and Margaret Edge. The entry for Margaret Webb states:

> Margaret *m*. Rev. James Davenport, D.D., Vicar of Stratford-upon-Avon, co. Warwick. *d.s.p.* 1796.

'd.s.p.' is an abbreviation for the Latin expression 'decessit sine prole' which means 'died without issue', but James and Margaret Davenport had four children following their marriage in 1791, and Margaret died three days after their last child was born. In 1808 James Davenport married a widow with the same name as his first wife, another Margaret Webb, widow of Thomas Webb, his first wife's cousin. This Margaret Webb was by then beyond childbearing age, and it is possible that the compiler of the pedigree confused these two women.

Various volumes of pedigrees and biographical directories were published in the late nineteenth and early twentieth centuries. *The County Families of the United Kingdom*, by Edward Walford, was published annually from 1860. A biography of Thomas Wilkins (1786–1875) appeared in the first volume:

WILKINS, Thomas, Esq.

Eldest son of the late Thomas Wilkins, Esq., of Stanwick, co. Northampton, by Mary, dau. of the Rev. Richard Haighton, Rector of Long Stow and Croxton, co. Cambridge ; *b.* 1786 ; *s.* 1813 ; *m.* 1st 1814 Elizabeth, heiress of Rev. Thomas Sheepshanks, Rector of Wimpole, co. Cambridge ; 2nd Augusta Sophia, dau. of James Dyson, Esq., of Bedford. Is a Magistrate and Dep. Lieut. for co. Northampton, and a Magistrate for Hunts and Warwickshire. This family is descended from Dr. John Wilkins, Bishop of Chester, who married Robinia Cromwell, a sister of the Protector.—Pelham Villa, near Leamington, Warwickshire.

Heir, his grandson Richard Haighton, *b.* 1851.

Extensive research in original sources has revealed a significant number of inaccuracies in this account:

• Thomas Wilkins's mother, Mary Haighton, was the daughter of Thomas Haighton of Baildon in Yorkshire, and not of the Reverend Richard Haighton, who was her uncle and died childless.

• The abbreviation '*s.*' denotes 'succeeded (to a title or estate)' but Thomas Wilkins's father died in 1839 and not in 1813.

• Thomas Wilkins was actually married three times, and the marriages listed are his second and third. His first marriage was to Naomi Woollard Wallis in 1810. She died in 1811, shortly after the birth of his eldest son, Richard Haighton Wilkins. His second marriage was in 1813 and not 1814.

• Elizabeth Sheepshanks was the only child of the Reverend Thomas Sheepshanks by his first wife, but she was not his heiress, as he had two sons by his second wife.

• There is no evidence that this family is descended from Dr John Wilkins, Bishop of Chester (1614–1672), whose father was an Oxfordshire goldsmith. Thomas Wilkins's father, referred to as 'Thomas Wilkins, Esq., of Stanwick', was born at Brackley in Northamptonshire where the ancestral line has been traced back through several previous generations to the early seventeenth century, and no connection to the Oxfordshire Wilkins family has been found. When John Wilkins married Robina (not Robinia) French, widow of Peter French and youngest sister of Oliver Cromwell, she was beyond childbearing age, and although it is possible that he had been married before, there is no evidence that he had any surviving children.

• Although Thomas Wilkins's heir was his grandson, this was not Richard Haighton Wilkins born in 1851, but Haighton Wilkins born in 1847, six months after the death of his father Richard Haighton Wilkins in a tragic accident.

The preface to 'Walford' states that the information in the publication was obtained as a result of both direct enquiries to the families concerned and 'private enquiries among local friends and correspondents, and by consulting a large library of useful books of reference'. Thomas Wilkins was alive in 1860 when the first volume was published, but the number of errors suggests that he was not the source of the information, which may have been put together from published sources such as the *Gentleman's Magazine* and various directories.

Many printed sources published during the Victorian and Edwardian periods are now out of copyright and have been digitized online, so the information they contain can often be found as a result of a simple Google search. Researchers may be inclined to believe that information originally published in printed sources of this type must be accurate because they superficially resemble other more authoritative reference works. Although much of the genealogical information in published pedigrees and biographical accounts is likely to be accurate, particularly for more recent generations, they contain many errors, so any information that is not supported by evidence or references to sources should be verified by further research.

Chapter 14

HELP FROM OTHERS

DISTANT RELATIVES

People with a common ancestor are related through siblings of the next generation whose lines of descent have subsequently diverged, to different places in the same area, to different areas within the British Isles, or to different countries, often on different continents. If a significant number of descendants of a person who lived in the pre-Victorian period are now living, there is a good chance that some of them will be researching their family history. Some distant relatives may have inherited old family papers and others may be serious researchers who have carried out a great deal of research in original sources. If two or more descendants are researching backwards towards a common ancestor by different routes, they may find items of information in sources that would be difficult or impossible for a single researcher to identify without a specific clue.

Contact with living descendants of an elusive sibling of a direct ancestor who apparently disappeared by migrating to another area or country can sometimes enable brick walls to be overcome, as records may exist in the destination area that complement those in the area of origin. Identifying and making contact with distant relatives is now much easier than it was in the past because many people have shared their family history information on the internet using services such as Ancestry, or on their own websites.

Information from other researchers can be very helpful, particularly if it is based on family papers or original research. However, many publicly available family trees are based exclusively on information found online, including information imported from other family trees, usually without any verification, and demonstrate little or no evidence of research using original sources that are not available online. Because so much information has been imported from the trees of others, when family trees are found that include promising information it may be difficult to establish the identity of the person who originally carried out the research or provided the information. Some people who previously made the results of their research available online may have since removed it and it is inevitable that some will have died. Nevertheless, if a living descendant of an ancestor can be identified, there may be the potential to overcome a brick wall through the sharing of information.

For each earlier generation the number of distant cousins increases. The larger pool of descendants of ancestors who lived in the pre-Victorian period may be particularly relevant to researching people who died or left the country just before the 1851 census, as memorabilia may still survive from the early nineteenth century. Family memorabilia are often passed down through subsequent generations quite randomly, and one living descendant may have inherited memorabilia going back many generations, while most or all other descendants have inherited nothing at all. An old family bible from the mid- or late nineteenth century could include details of several earlier generations that would be difficult or impossible to establish based entirely on information available in public records.

LOCAL HISTORY SOCIETIES AND LOCAL HISTORIANS
If an individual or family is known to have lived in a specific hamlet or village, contacting a local history society may enable people with expert knowledge of the locality to be identified. Some local historians may have collected a considerable amount of information on the locality they are interested in, and identified documents, such as deeds, which may not be listed separately in the catalogue of the archives where they are held. Local historians may also welcome contact with genealogical researchers who can supply them with information about people who lived in the locality from other sources.

ONE-NAME STUDIES

When carrying out research on a family with an uncommon surname, there is the possibility that a one-name study is in progress and that a considerable amount of information from different sources has already been collected. One-name studies have often been started by family history researchers in the hope that by reconstituting all the identifiable families with the surname of interest they will be able to make further progress in their own research. Many people carrying out one-name studies are members of the Guild of One-Name Studies, but others who are not members have set up websites, and family history societies have been established for some surnames. The Alderson Family History Society, for example, has almost 300 members throughout the world, most of whom are descended from families who lived in Swaledale in the North Riding of Yorkshire in the sixteenth and seventeenth centuries, where many people with the surname still live today.

IN-HOUSE RESEARCH SERVICES

Archive services routinely answer enquiries relating to the records they hold, and many are willing to carry out quick look-ups in card indexes and other search tools only available on the premises at no charge. For anything more than this it is usually necessary either to visit the relevant archive to carry out research in person or to pay to have research carried out. If it is decided to pay for research, there may be a choice between employing an independent local researcher or using an archive service's own in-house research service if they provide one. In the latter case, there is often a limit to the number of hours spent on each enquiry, so employing an independent researcher may be the only option for extended research. On the other hand, most in-house research services will carry out small research tasks, often charging in blocks of 15 or 30 minutes, whereas independent researchers often have a minimum charge based on at least one hour's work. Paid research in larger archives is rarely carried out by professional archivists, and the grades and skills of the staff who handle such enquiries varies. Some archive services employ dedicated researchers, who may have skills similar to those of independent professional genealogists. Many small specialist archives have only one member of staff, often a professional archivist with considerable knowledge of the record collections, who may be able to identify further sources containing genealogical information that independent researchers are less likely to be aware of. The hourly charges for research in archives vary considerably, but archive services are obliged to charge VAT, so charges for in-house research services are often higher than those of self-employed independent researchers.

PROFESSIONAL GENEALOGISTS AND RECORD SEARCHERS

There are several reasons why people researching their own ancestors might consider paying others to carry out research:

• They are having difficulty reading and understanding certain records.
• Archives where relevant sources are located are too far away for personal research to be practicable.
• They require research to be coordinated in several different archives in the same local area.
• They hope that an experienced professional will be able to solve a genealogical problem when they have hit a brick wall.

Many people advertise paid research services, some focusing on searching records in specific archives and others offering comprehensive genealogical research services. Until relatively recently there was a recognized distinction between the two roles of professional genealogist and record agent, although in practice it was common for one person to perform both functions. A genealogist acted as a consultant, establishing a research strategy, directing the research, carrying out some research personally, delegating searching of specific sources to local record agents where necessary, and finally reporting back to the client. A record agent searched specific sources that had been identified by the genealogist.

The description of people as record agents is now rarely used, but the distinction between these two complementary activities still remains, as each requires slightly different knowledge and skills. Effective genealogical research requires knowledge of a wide range of sources and research techniques, and the ability to see the 'big picture'. Effective searching of specific sources requires detailed knowledge of each source, including the ability to read any distinctive styles of handwriting and to understand the significance of specific terms and abbreviations.

When selecting someone to carry out paid research the choice may be influenced by whether the work is restricted to searching specific sources that have already been identified or involves trying to overcome a brick wall. Many people offering to carry out paid research for clients describe themselves as professional genealogists or genealogical experts and often have considerable experience of searching certain types of source located in specific archives, but they may not have the more comprehensive knowledge of sources, both local and national, or the analytical and problem-solving skills that become increasingly important for finding solutions to genealogical problems in the pre-Victorian period. Genealogy as a profession is unregulated, so although some researchers without formal qualifications are extremely competent, often as a result of previous employment in archives, the knowledge and experience of others may be more limited. Apart from personal recommendation, it is only possible to gauge the competence of an independent researcher if their knowledge and ability have been independently assessed.

In many professions the description 'professional' implies not only the possession of a qualification obtained as a result of study and formal assessment but also further accreditation by a professional body. Recognizing that many potential clients wish to employ professional genealogists fulfilling similar criteria, an increasing number of people wishing to carry out paid research for clients invest time, money and effort in obtaining advanced qualifications in genealogy and in becoming Members of AGRA, the only organization for professional genealogists in England and Wales to require evidence of competence as a condition of membership. AGRA was established in 1968 as the Association of Genealogists and Record Agents, but the name was changed in 2001 to the Association of Genealogists and Researchers in Archives. Some professional genealogists, whether or not they are also AGRA Members, have obtained postgraduate-level qualifications in genealogy from the IHGS (Institute of Heraldic and Genealogical Studies) in Canterbury and from the universities of Strathclyde and Dundee in Scotland. Some people offering paid research services in England are members of the American-based Association of Professional Genealogists (APG), but unlike AGRA there is no requirement to submit any evidence of competence as a condition of membership.

The fees charged by professional genealogists who have relevant advanced qualifications or who are AGRA Members are likely to be higher than those of unqualified or unaccredited researchers. Experienced professional genealogists with demonstrable track records may charge more than those who have only recently started offering a professional research service. Although they may charge a higher hourly rate, experienced professionals may be able to find elusive information and overcome difficult brick walls that would defeat many unqualified or less experienced researchers.

BIBLIOGRAPHY

Alcock, N.W. (2001) *Old Title Deeds: A Guide for Local and Family Historians*. 2nd ed. Chichester: Phillimore.

Anderson, R.C. (2014) *Elements of Genealogical Analysis*. Boston: New England Historical Genealogical Society.

Bevan, A. (2006) *Tracing Your Ancestors in the National Archives*. 7th ed. Kew: National Archives.

Board for Certification of Genealogists (2000) *The BCG Genealogical Standards Manual*. New York: Turner.

Burn, J.S. (1829) *The History of Parish Registers in England*. London: Edward Suter.

Chambers, P. (2006) *Early Modern Genealogy: Researching Your Family History 1600–1838*. Stroud: Sutton.

Cole, J. and Titford, J. (2003) *Tracing Your Family Tree*. 4th ed. Newbury: Countryside Books.

Erickson, A.L. (2012) *Mistresses and Marriage: Or, a Short History of the Mrs.* (Working Papers from Department of Economic and Social History at the University of Cambridge, No. 8.) Available from: http://EconPapers.repec.org/RePEc:cmh:wpaper:06

Gardner, D.E. and Smith, F. (1964) *Genealogical Research in England and Wales. Volume 3: Old English Handwriting, Latin, Research Standards and Procedures*. Salt Lake City: Bookcraft.

Gibson, J. and Raymond, S. (2016) *Probate Jurisdictions: Where to Look for Wills*. 6th ed. Bury: The Family History Partnership.

Guildhall Library. (1995) *The British Overseas: A Guide to Records of their Births, Baptisms, Marriages, Deaths and Burials, Available in the United Kingdom*. 3rd ed. London: Guildhall Library.

Hawkings, D.T. (2011) *Pauper Ancestors: A Guide to the Records Created by the Poor Laws in England and Wales*. Stroud: History Press.

Herber, M. (2004) *Ancestral Trails*. 2nd ed. Stroud: Sutton.

Humphery-Smith, C.R. (2003) *The Phillimore Atlas and Index of Parish Registers*. 3rd ed. Chichester: Phillimore.

Marshall, H. (2004) *Palaeography for Local and Family Historians*. 2nd ed. Chichester: Phillimore.

Mills, E.S. (2015) *Evidence Explained: Citing History Sources from Artifacts to Cyberspace*. 2nd ed. Baltimore: Genealogical Publishing Company.

Oates, J. (2012) *Tracing Your Ancestors from 1066 to 1837*. Barnsley: Pen & Sword.

Osborn, H. (2012) *Genealogy: Essential Research Methods*. London: Robert Hale.

Paley, R. (2011) *My Ancestor was a Bastard*. London: Society of Genealogists.

Probert, R. (2012) *Marriage Law for Genealogists*. Kenilworth: Takeaway.

Raymond, S.A. (2010) *My Ancestor was an Apprentice*. London: Society of Genealogists.

Raymond, S.A. (2012) *The Wills of our Ancestors*. Barnsley: Pen & Sword.

Rogers, C.D. (2008) *The Family Tree Detective*. 4th ed. Manchester: Manchester University Press.

Steel, D.J. (1973) *Sources for Nonconformist Genealogy and Family History* (National Index of Parish Registers, Volume 2.) Chichester: Phillimore.

Tate, W.E. (2011) *The Parish Chest: A Study of the Records of Parochial Administration in England*. 3rd ed. Stroud: History Press.

Todd, A. (2015) *Family History Nuts and Bolts: Problem-Solving through Family Reconstitution Techniques*. 3rd ed. Ramsbottom: Andrew Todd.

Wagner, A. (1983) *English Genealogy*. 2nd ed. Chichester: Phillimore.

Whyte, I.D. (2000) *Migration and Society in Britain, 1550–1830*. Basingstoke: Macmillan.

Wormleighton, T. (2012) *Title Deeds for Family Historians*. Bury: The Family History Partnership.

INDEX